GW00708682

LONGMANS' ENGLISH CLASSICS

EDITED BY

ASHLEY H. THORNDIKE, Ph.D., L.H.D.

PROFESSOR OF ENGLISH IN COLUMBIA UNIVERSITY

THOMAS GRAY

THE ELEGY AND OTHER POEMS

OLIVER GOLDSMITH

THE DESERTED VILLAGE, THE TRAVELLER
AND OTHER POEMS

Longmans' English Classics

THOMAS GRAY'S

ELEGY

WRITTEN IN A COUNTRY CHURCHYARD

AND OTHER POEMS

———

OLIVER GOLDSMITH'S

THE DESERTED VILLAGE
THE TRAVELLER

AND OTHER POEMS

EDITED

WITH NOTES AND AN INTRODUCTION BY

JAMES F. HOSIC, Ph.M.

EAD OF THE DEPARTMENT OF ENGLISH IN THE CHICAGO NORMAL COLLEGE

NEW YORK

LONGMANS, GREEN, AND CO.

LONDON, BOMBAY, AND CALCUTTA

1910

THE SCIENTIFIC PRESS
ROBERT DRUMMOND AND COMPANY
NEW YORK

CONTENTS

———

INTRODUCTION

GRAY and Goldsmith were contemporaries. Born in the so-called Age of Pope, both lived well on into the period of English letters dominated by Samuel Johnson. The works of both give indications of the dawning romanticism which was to result in the period of Wordsworth and Scott. Both were writers of fluent and admirable prose as well as poets. And there are some personal resemblances. Both found the prescribed work of college, especially mathematics, distasteful, and preferred to read at will; both travelled extensively on the continent; neither married. But the likenesses between the two are few and mainly superficial. In temperament, in experience, in kind and quantity of work, our authors were very different. Gray was a sober, retiring scholar, who lived by choice within college walls near the great libraries, shrinking from notoriety and cherishing a few friends with intellectual sympathies like his own. He was a painstaking student, devoted to knowledge for its own sake, keenly critical, and loth to publish his literary efforts to the world. Goldsmith, on the other hand, was convivial to a degree. He loved the society of his fellows, even the humblest and the rudest, and was warmly loved by them in return. His parents were poor. He himself was the victim of chronic improvidence and of a soft heart, which refused no demand upon his charity; so that he was unable, like Gray, to live the life of a gentleman reading for pleasure. After many fruitless adventures he settled in the heart of London and slaved for the booksellers to earn his daily bread. Hack work, however, could not wholly stifle his genius. He became a member of the Literary Club and an intimate of Johnson, Garrick, Burke, and Reynolds. He wrote the *Traveller*, the *Deserted Village*, the *Vicar of Wakefield*, *She Stoops to Conquer;* and before his death he had gained much of the recognition and popularity he sought.

We must read the poems of these two writers, then, from somewhat different points of view. The interest in Gray must inevitably be largely in his method. He was a conscious literary experimenter and very sensitive to all the intellectual currents and counter-currents of his times. His odes, for example, are clever attempts to carry Greek and Italian models over into English verse. As a whole, his work represents three distinct periods of development, in each of which a particular interest predominates. He began as a classicist, an avowed admirer of Dryden and Pope; with the *Elegy* he joined the followers of Milton; and finally he became a student of early Norse and Welsh literature and wrote poems based upon these sources. All his work shows the greatest familiarity with classic writers, especially the poets, both of England and of Italy and Greece. He has the scholar's fondness for remote allusion, and he echoes, often consciously, many memorable phrases from the authors he knew so well. With the exception of the *Elegy*, the human interest is not strong in Gray, and even in that poem the experience is broadly typical. It holds us rather by its exquisite poetic tone and perfect expression than by the appeal of the emotion. We shall do well, therefore, to read Gray's poems with an eye to his excellence in the art of verse, his spoils of many a literary conquest, and the reflection of influences that he helped to pass on. This is the sort of material which repays careful study.

As has been indicated above, we approach Goldsmith with other expectations. True, he has a delightfully easy and graceful style, but this everyone will readily feel who will take the trouble to read his poems aloud. There is little of the scholar's erudition or the critic's nicety. His plan is simple and simply carried out. There is nothing either subtle or profound. But always there is sympathy with life and always the charm and pathos which the character of Goldsmith so remarkably combined. We read the *Traveller* and the *Deserted Village*, not for the truth of their pictures of social conditions nor their more than doubtful political economy, but for the amiable spirit which animates them, for the kindly personality they reflect. As Irving says: "We read his character in every page and grow into familiar intimacy with him as we read. The artless benevolence that beams throughout his works; the whimsical yet amiable views of human life and human nature; the unforced humour, blending so happily with good-feeling and good-sense, and singularly dashed at times with a pleasing melancholy; even the very nature of his mellow and flowing and softly-tinted style—all seem to bespeak his moral as well as his intellectual qualities, and make us love the man at the same time that we admire the author."

BIBLIOGRAPHICAL NOTE

GRAY's Complete Works, including his Letters, are edited by Edmund Gosse. There is an excellent volume of selections of both verse and prose in the *Athenæum Press Series*, edited by William Lyon Phelps. This contains a bibliography. The standard life of Gray is by Edmund Gosse in the *English Men of Letters Series*, new edition in 1889. The most important essays are by Matthew Arnold in Ward's *English Poets*, vol. iii; by Lowell in his *Latest Literary Essays;* by Austin Dobson in *Eighteenth Century Vignettes*; and by Leslie Stephen in *Hours in a Library*. The authoritative text of Gray's poems is Dodsley's, published in 1768, and corrected by Gray himself. The most important manuscript is the Pembroke MS., found among Gray's papers after his death.

Goldsmith's Works were edited by Peter Cunningham in 1854. Later editions are the *Bohn* in five volumes, by J. W. M. Gibbs; *Poems, Plays and Essays* by J. Aikin and H. T. Tuckerman; and *Miscellaneous Works* with a Memoir by David Masson—the Globe edition. The standard life of Goldsmith is that by J. Forster, which has passed through several editions. Irving's more literary account is based on this. The Goldsmith number of the *English Men of Letters Series*, by William Black, is excellent. Other biographies are by A. Dobson in the *Great Writers*

Series, Wm. M. Rossetti in *Lives of Famous Poets,* and
Elbert Hubbard in *Little Journeys to the Homes of Good
Men and Great.* There are, of course, many references to
Goldsmith in Boswell's *Johnson,* but they are generally
inspired by jealousy. The principal essays are by Macaulay,
by Thackeray in his *English Humorists,* by DeQuincey in
Essays on the Poets, and by Dobson in his *Miscellanies.*

Among the important works dealing with the literary
period to which Gray and Goldsmith ·belong, Perry's
English Literature in the Eighteenth Century, Gosse's
Eighteenth Century Literature, Phelps's *Beginning of the
English Romantic Movement,* and Beers's *English Romanticism in the Eighteenth Century,* are perhaps the most
useful. Besant's *London in the Eighteenth Century* should
also be consulted.

CHRONOLOGICAL TABLE

GRAY AND GOLDSMITH.	CONTEMPORARY LITERARY HISTORY.
1716. Gray born, Dec. 26.	
	1717. Horace Walpole born. Pope's *Eloisa to Abelard*.
	1719. Addison died. Defoe's *Robinson Crusoe*, Part I.
	1721. Smollett born. Collins born.
	1725. Ramsay's *Gentle Shepherd*.
	1726. Swift's *Gulliver's Travels*.
	1726–30. Thomson's *Seasons*.
1728. Goldsmith born, Nov. 10.	1728. Gay's *Beggar's Opera*. Pope's *Dunciad*.
	1729. Burke born. Steele died. Congreve died.
	1730. Pope and others: *The Grub Street Journal*.
	1731. Cowper born. Defoe died.
	1732–34. Pope's *Essay on Man*.
	1732. Gay died.
1734. Gray entered Peterhouse, Cambridge.	
	1736. Butler's *Analogy of Religion*.
	1737. Shenstone's *Schoolmistress*. Gibbon born.
	1738. Johnson's *London*.
1739. Gray traveled on the Continent with Horace Walpole.	
	1740. Richardson's *Pamela*.
1741. Gray's father died.	

CHRONOLOGICAL TABLE—*Continued*

GRAY AND GOLDSMITH.	CONTEMPORARY LITERARY HISTORY.
1742. Gray settled down at Cambridge; wrote *Ode on the Spring, Eton Ode, Hymn to Adversity.*	1742. Fielding's *Joseph Andrews.*
	1742–44. Young's *Night Thoughts.*
1744. Goldsmith entered Trinity College, Dublin.	1744. Akenside's *Pleasures of the Imagination.* Chesterfield's *Letters to his Son.* Pope died.
	1745. Swift died.
	1746. Collins's *Odes.*
1747. Gray's *Ode on the Death of a Favourite Cat.*	
	1748. Richardson's *Clarissa Harlowe.* Smollett's *Roderick Random.* Thomson's *Castle of Indolence.*
1749. Goldsmith took his B.A. degree.	1749. Fielding's *Tom Jones.*
	1750. Johnson's *Rambler.*
1751. Gray's *Elegy* (written 1742–1750).	1751. Sheridan born.
1752–54. Goldsmith a medical student in Edinburgh.	1752. Frances Burney born. Chatterton born.
1753. Gray's *Six Poems.*	1753–61. Hume's *History of England.*
1754–56. Goldsmith traveled and studied on the Continent.	1754. Fielding died. Crabbe born.
1754. Gray wrote *Progress of Poesy.*	
	1755. Johnson's *Dictionary of the English Language.*
	1756. Burke's *Our Ideas of the Sublime and Beautiful.*
1757. Gray's *Pindaric Odes.* Goldsmith engaged to do hackwork for Griffiths the publisher.	1757. Blake born. Dyer's *Fleece.*
	1758. Johnson's *Idler.*
1759. Goldsmith's *Enquiry into the Present State of Polite Learning in Europe, The Bee;* made the acquaintance of Johnson.	1759. Johnson's *Rasselas.* Sterne's *Tristram Shandy.* Burns born.
	1759–69. Sir Joshua Reynolds' Essays in the *Idler.*

CHRONOLOGICAL TABLE—*Continued*

GRAY AND GOLDSMITH.	CONTEMPORARY LITERARY HISTORY.
1760. Goldsmith's *Citizen of the World*.	1760. Macpherson's *Fragments of Ancient Poetry*.
1761. Goldsmith's *Memoirs of M. de Voltaire*.	1761. Smollett's Translation of Le Sage's *Gil Blas*.
1762. Goldsmith's *Life of Mr. Richard Nash*.	1762. Macpherson's *Poems of Ossian*.
1764. Goldsmith's *Traveller* (begun in 1755).	1764. Walpole's *Castle of Otranto*.
1765. Goldsmith's *Essays, Edwin and Angelina, History of England in a Series of Letters*. He became a member of the Literary Club.	1765. Percy's *Reliques of Ancient English Poetry*.
1766. Goldsmith's *Vicar of Wakefield* (probably written in 1762). *Poems for Young Ladies*.	
	1767. Maria Edgeworth born.
1768. Goldsmith's *Good-Natur'd Man*. Standard edition of Gray's *Poems*. Elected Professor of Modern History at Cambridge.	1768. Sterne's *Sentimental Journey*.
1769. Gray's *Ode for Music, Journal in the Lakes*. Goldsmith's *Roman History*.	
1770. Goldsmith's *Deserted Village, Life of Parnell, Life of Bolingbroke*. Elected Professor of History to the Royal Academy; made a visit to Paris.	1770. Wordsworth born. Burke's *Thoughts on the Present Discontents*. Akenside died.
1771. Goldsmith's *History of England*. Gray died, July 30.	1771. Scott born. Smollett's *Humphrey Clinker*. Smollett died.
	1772. Coleridge born. *Junius Letters*.
1773. Goldsmith's *She Stoops to Conquer*.	
1774. Goldsmith died, April 4. *Retaliation* published, April 9. *History of Animated Nature* in June.	1774. Mason's *Life of Gray*. Southey born.

CHRONOLOGICAL TABLE—*Continued*

GRAY AND GOLDSMITH.	CONTEMPORARY LITERARY HISTORY.
1776. Goldsmith's *Haunch of Venison*.	1775. Sheridan's *Rivals* and *Duenna*. Jane Austen born. Lamb born. Landor born. 1777. Sheridan's *School for Scandal*. 1778. Miss Burney's *Evelina*. Hazlitt born. 1779. Johnson's *Lives of the Poets*. 1783. Crabbe's *The Village*. 1784. Johnson died.

THOMAS GRAY

THE ELEGY AND OTHER POEMS

ELEGY

WRITTEN IN A COUNTRY CHURCH-YARD

The curfew tolls the knell of parting day,
  The lowing herd wind slowly o'er the lea,
The plowman homeward plods his weary way,
  And leaves the world to darkness and to me.

Now fades the glimmering landscape on the sight,   5
  And all the air a solemn stillness holds,
Save where the beetle wheels his droning flight,
  And drowsy tinklings lull the distant folds;

Save that from yonder ivy-mantled tow'r,
  The moping owl does to the moon complain   10
Of such as, wand'ring near her secret bow'r,
  Molest her ancient solitary reign.

Beneath those rugged elms, that yew-tree's shade,
  Where heaves the turf in many a mould'ring heap,
Each in his narrow cell forever laid,   15
  The rude forefathers of the hamlet sleep.

The breezy call of incense-breathing Morn,
  The swallow twitt'ring from the straw-built shed,
The cock's shrill clarion, or the echoing horn,
  No more shall rouse them from their lowly bed.   20

For them no more the blazing hearth shall burn,
　Or busy housewife ply her evening care;
No children run to lisp their sire's return,
　Or climb his knees the envied kiss to share.

Oft did the harvest to their sickle yield,　　　　　　25
　Their furrow oft the stubborn glebe has broke;
How jocund did they drive their team afield!
　How bow'd the woods beneath their sturdy stroke!

Let not Ambition mock their useful toil,
　Their homely joys, and destiny obscure;　　　　　30
Nor Grandeur hear with a disdainful smile
　The short and simple annals of the poor.

The boast of heraldry, the pomp of pow'r,
　And all that beauty, all that wealth e'er gave,
Await alike th' inevitable hour.　　　　　　　35
　The paths of glory lead but to the grave.

Nor you, ye proud, impute to these the fault,
　If Mem'ry o'er their tomb no trophies raise,
Where through the long-drawn aisle and fretted vault
　The pealing anthem swells the note of praise.　　40

Can storied urn, or animated bust,
　Back to its mansion call the fleeting breath?
Can Honour's voice provoke the silent dust,
　Or Flatt'ry soothe the dull cold ear of Death?

Perhaps in this neglected spot is laid　　　　　　45
　Some heart once pregnant with celestial fire,
Hands, that the rod of empire might have sway'd,
　Or wak'd to ecstasy the living lyre.

But Knowledge to their eyes her ample page
   Rich with the spoils of time did ne'er unroll;   50
Chill Penury repress'd their noble rage,
   And froze the genial current of the soul.

Full many a gem of purest ray serene
   The dark unfathom'd caves of ocean bear;
Full many a flower is born to blush unseen,   55
   And waste its sweetness on the desert air.

Some village Hampden, that with dauntless breast
   The little Tyrant of his fields withstood,
Some mute inglorious Milton here may rest,
   Some Cromwell guiltless of his country's blood.   60

Th' applause of list'ning senates to command,
   The threats of pain and ruin to despise,
To scatter plenty o'er a smiling land,
   And read their hist'ry in a nation's eyes,

Their lot forbade: nor circumscrib'd alone   65
   Their growing virtues, but their crimes confin'd;
Forbade to wade through slaughter to a throne,
   And shut the gates of mercy on mankind;

The struggling pangs of conscious truth to hide,
   To quench the blushes of ingenuous shame,   70
Or heap the shrine of Luxury and Pride
   With incense kindled at the Muse's flame.

Far from the madding crowd's ignoble strife,
   Their sober wishes never learn'd to stray;
Along the cool sequester'd vale of life   75
   They kept the noiseless tenor of their way.

Yet ev'n these bones from insult to protect
    Some frail memorial still erected nigh,
With uncouth rhymes and shapeless sculpture deck'd
    Implores the passing tribute of a sigh.   80

Their name, their years, spelt by th' unletter'd Muse,
    The place of fame and elegy supply;
And many a holy text around she strews,
    That teach the rustic moralist to die.

For who, to dumb Forgetfulness a prey,   85
    This pleasing anxious being e'er resigned,
Left the warm precincts of the cheerful day,
    Nor cast one longing, ling'ring look behind?

On some fond breast the parting soul relies,
    Some pious drops the closing eye requires;   90
E'en from the tomb the voice of Nature cries,
    E'en in our ashes live their wonted fires.

For thee, who, mindful of th' unhonour'd dead,
    Dost in these lines their artless tale relate;
If chance, by lonely contemplation led,   95
    Some kindred spirit shall enquire thy fate,—

Haply some hoary-headed swain may say,
    "Oft have we seen him at the peep of dawn
Brushing with hasty steps the dews away,
    To meet the sun upon the upland lawn: 100

"There at the foot of yonder nodding beech,
    That wreathes its old fantastic roots so high,
His listless length at noontide would he stretch,
    And pore upon the brook that babbles by.

"Hard by yon wood, now smiling as in scorn,   105
   Mutt'ring his wayward fancies he would rove;
Now drooping, woeful-wan, like one forlorn,
   Or craz'd with care, or cross'd in hopeless love.

"One morn I miss'd him on the custom'd hill,
   Along the heath, and near his fav'rite tree;   110
Another came; nor yet beside the rill,
   Nor up the lawn, nor at the wood was he;

'The next, with dirges due in sad array,
   Slow through the church-way path we saw him borne.—
Approach and read (for thou can'st read) the lay   115
   Grav'd on the stone beneath yon aged thorn."

THE EPITAPH

Here rests his head upon the lap of Earth,
   A youth, to Fortune and to Fame unknown:
Fair Science frown'd not on his humble birth,
   And Melancholy mark'd him for her own.   120

Large was his bounty, and his soul sincere,
   Heav'n did a recompense as largely send;
He gave to Mis'ry all he had, a tear,
   He gain'd from Heav'n ('twas all he wish'd) a friend.

No farther seek his merits to disclose,   125
   Or draw his frailties from their dread abode,
(There they alike in trembling hope repose,)
   The bosom of his Father and his God.

ODE ON A DISTANT PROSPECT OF ETON COLLEGE

Ἄνθρωπος, ἱκανὴ πρόφασις εἰς τὸ δυστυχεῖν.
MENANDER.

YE distant spires, ye antique towers,
　That crown the wat'ry glade,
Where grateful Science still adores
　Her Henry's holy shade;
And ye, that from the stately brow　　　　　　5
Of Windsor's heights th' expanse below
　Of grove, of lawn, of mead survey,
Whose turf, whose shade, whose flowers among
Wanders the hoary Thames along
　His silver-winding way:　　　　　　　　　10

Ah, happy hills! ah, pleasing shade!
　Ah, fields belov'd in vain!
Where once my careless childhood stray'd,
　A stranger yet to pain!
I feel the gales that from ye blow　　　　　　15
A momentary bliss bestow,
　As waving fresh their gladsome wing
My weary soul they seem to soothe,
And, redolent of joy and youth,
　To breathe a second spring.　　　　　　　20

Say, Father Thames, for thou hast seen
　Full many a sprightly race
Disporting on thy margent green,
　The paths of pleasure trace,

Who foremost now delight to cleave   25
With pliant arm thy glassy wave?
   The captive linnet which enthral?
What idle progeny succeed
To chase the rolling circle's speed,
   Or urge the flying ball?   30

While some on earnest business bent
   Their murm'ring labours ply
'Gainst graver hours, that bring constraint
   To sweeten liberty:
Some bold adventurers disdain   35
The limits of their little reign,
   And unknown regions dare descry:
Still as they run they look behind,
They hear a voice in every wind,
   And snatch a fearful joy.   40

Gay hope is theirs by fancy fed,
   Less pleasing when possest;
The tear forgot as soon as shed,
   The sunshine of the breast:
Theirs buxom health of rosy hue,   45
Wild wit, invention ever new,
   And lively cheer of vigour born;
The thoughtless day, the easy night,
The spirits pure, the slumbers light,
   That fly th' approach of morn.   50

Alas! regardless of their doom
   The little victims play;
No sense have they of ills to come,
   Nor care beyond to-day:

Yet see, how all around 'em wait   55
The ministers of human fate,
    And black Misfortune's baleful train!
Ah, shew them where in ambush stand,
To seize their prey, the murth'rous band!
    Ah, tell them, they are men!   60

These shall the fury Passions tear,
    The vultures of the mind,
Disdainful Anger, pallid Fear,
    And Shame that skulks behind;
Or pining Love shall waste their youth,   65
Or Jealousy with rankling tooth
    That inly gnaws the secret heart;
And Envy wan, and faded Care,
Grim-visag'd comfortless Despair,
    And Sorrow's piercing dart.   70

Ambition this shall tempt to rise,
    Then whirl the wretch from high,
To bitter Scorn a sacrifice,
    And grinning Infamy.
The stings of Falsehood those shall try,   75
And hard Unkindness' alter'd eye,
    That mocks the tear it forc'd to flow;
And keen Remorse with blood defil'd,
And moody Madness laughing wild
    Amid severest woe.   80

Lo! in the vale of years beneath
    A grisly troop are seen,
The painful family of Death,
    More hideous than their queen:

This racks the joints, this fires the veins,　　　85
That every labouring sinew strains,
　　Those in the deeper vitals rage:
Lo! Poverty, to fill the band,
That numbs the soul with icy hand,
　　And slow-consuming Age.　　　　　90

To each his suff'rings: all are men,
　　Condemn'd alike to groan;
The tender for another's pain,
　　Th' unfeeling for his own.
Yet, ah! why should they know their fate,　　95
Since sorrow never comes too late,
　　And happiness too swiftly flies?
Thought would destroy their paradise.
No more;—where ignorance is bliss,
　　'Tis folly to be wise.　　　　　100

ODE ON THE DEATH OF A FAVOURITE CAT

DROWNED IN A TUB OF GOLD FISHES

'TWAS on a lofty vase's side,
Where China's gayest art had dy'd
　　The azure flowers that blow;
Demurest of the tabby kind,
　　The pensive Selima reclin'd,　　　5
Gaz'd on the lake below.

Her conscious tail her joy declar'd;
The fair round face, the snowy beard,
　　The velvet of her paws,

Her coat, that with the tortoise vies,   10
Her ears of jet, and emerald eyes,
    She saw; and purr'd applause.

Still had she gaz'd; but 'midst the tide
Two angel forms were seen to glide,
    The Genii of the stream: 15
Their scaly armour's Tyrian hue
Thro' richest purple to the view
    Betray'd a golden gleam.

The hapless Nymph with wonder saw:
A whisker first and then a claw,   20
    With many an ardent wish,
She stretch'd in vain to reach the prize.
What female heart can gold despise?
    What Cat's averse to fish?

Presumptuous maid! with looks intent   25
Again she stretch'd, again she bent,
    Nor knew the gulf between.
(Malignant Fate sat by, and smil'd.)
The slipp'ry verge her feet beguil'd,
    She tumbled headlong in.   30

Eight times emerging from the flood,
She mew'd to ev'ry wat'ry God,
    Some speedy aid to send.
No Dolphin came, no Nereid stirr'd:
Nor cruel Tom, nor Susan heard.   35
    A fav'rite has no friend!

From hence, ye beauties, undeceiv'd,
Know, one false step is ne'er retriev'd,

And be with caution bold.
Not all that tempts your wand'ring eyes   40
And heedless hearts, is lawful prize,
    Nor all that glisters gold.

THE PROGRESS OF POESY

A PINDARIC ODE

Φωνᾶντα συνετοῖσιν·   ἐς
Δὲ τὸ πᾶν ἑρμηνέων
Χατίζει.

PINDAR, *Olympiad* II. v. 152.

I. I.

AWAKE, Æolian lyre, awake,
And give to rapture all thy trembling strings.
From Helicon's harmonious springs
    A thousand rills their mazy progress take:
The laughing flowers, that round them blow,   5
Drink life and fragrance as they flow.
Now the rich stream of music winds along,
Deep, majestic, smooth, and strong,
Thro' verdant vales, and Ceres' golden reign;
Now rolling down the steep amain,   10
Headlong, impetuous, see it pour;
The rocks and nodding groves rebellow to the roar.

I. 2.

Oh! Sov'reign of the willing soul,
Parent of sweet and solemn-breathing airs,
Enchanting shell! the sullen Cares   15
    And frantic Passions hear thy soft control.

On Thracia's hills the Lord of War
Has curb'd the fury of his car,
And dropt his thirsty lance at thy command.
Perching on the sceptred hand   20
Of Jove, thy magic lulls the feather'd king
With ruffled plumes and flagging wing:
Quench'd in dark clouds of slumber lie
The terrors of his beak, and lightnings of his eye.

I. 3.

Thee the voice, the dance, obey,   25
Temper'd to thy warbled lay.
O'er Idalia's velvet-green
The rosy-crownèd Loves are seen
On Cytherea's day
With antic Sport, and blue-eyed Pleasures,   30
Frisking light in frolic measures;
Now pursuing, now retreating,
   Now in circling troops they meet:
To brisk notes in cadence beating,
   Glance their many-twinkling feet.   35
Slow melting strains their Queen's approach declare:
   Where'er she turns, the Graces homage pay.
With arms sublime, that float upon the air.
   In gliding state she wins her easy way: .
O'er her warm cheek, and rising bosom, move   40
The bloom of young Desire and purple light of Love.

II. 1.

Man's feeble race what ills await!
Labour, and Penury, the racks of Pain.
Disease, and Sorrow's weeping train,

And Death, sad refuge from the storms of Fate!   45
The fond complaint, my song, disprove,
And justify the laws of Jove.
Say, has he giv'n in vain the heav'nly Muse?
Night, and all her sickly dews,
Her spectres wan, and birds of boding cry,   50
He gives to range the dreary sky;
Till down the eastern cliffs afar
Hyperion's march they spy, and glitt'ring shafts of war.

II. 2.

In climes beyond the solar road,
Where shaggy forms o'er ice-built mountains roam,   55
The Muse has broke the twilight-gloom
    To cheer the shiv'ring native's dull abode.
And oft, beneath the od'rous shade
Of Chili's boundless forests laid,
She deigns to hear the savage youth repeat,   60
In loose numbers wildly sweet,
Their feather-cinctur'd chiefs and dusky loves.
Her track, where'er the goddess roves,
Glory pursue, and generous Shame,
Th' unconquerable Mind, and freedom's holy flame.   65

II. 3.

Woods, that wave o'er Delphi's steep,
Isles that crown th' Ægean deep,
    Fields, that cool Ilissus laves,
    Or where Mæander's amber waves
In lingering lab'rinths creep,   70
    How do your tuneful echoes languish,
    Mute, but to the voice of anguish!

Where each old poetic mountain
   Inspiration breath'd around;
Ev'ry shade and hallow'd fountain   75
   Murmur'd deep⸜a solemn sound:
Till the sad Nine, in Greece's evil hour,
   Left their Parnassus for the Latian plains.
Alike they scorn the pomp of tyrant Power,
   And coward Vice, that revels in her chains.   80
When Latium had her lofty spirit lost,
They sought, oh Albion! next thy sea-encircled coast.

III. 1.

Far from the sun and summer-gale,
In thy green lap was Nature's darling laid,
What time, where lucid Avon stray'd,   85
   To him the mighty mother did unveil
Her awful face: the dauntless child
Stretch'd forth his little arms and smiled.
"This pencil take (she said), whose colours clear
Richly paint the vernal year: 90
Thine too these golden keys, immortal Boy
This can unlock the gates of Joy;
Of Horror that, and thrilling Fears,
Or ope the sacred source of sympathetic tears."

III. 2.

Nor second He, that rode sublime   95
Upon the seraph-wings of Ecstasy,
The secrets of th' Abyss to spy.
   He pass'd the flaming bounds of Place and Time:
The living throne, the sapphire blaze,
Where angels tremble while they gaze,   100

He saw; but, blasted with excess of light,
Clos'd his eyes in endless night.
Behold, where Dryden's less presumptuous car
Wide o'er the fields of glory bear
Two coursers of ethereal race,   105
With necks in thunder cloth'd, and long-resounding pace.

III. 3.

Hark, his hands the lyre explore!
Bright-eyed Fancy, hov'ring o'er,
Scatters from her pictur'd urn
Thoughts that breathe, and words that burn.   110
But ah! 't is heard no more—
    Oh! Lyre divine, what daring Spirit
    Wakes thee now? Tho' he inherit
Nor the pride, nor ample pinion,
    That the Theban eagle bear,   115
Sailing with supreme dominion
    Thro' the azure deep of air:
Yet oft before his infant eyes would run
    Such forms as glitter in the Muse's ray,
With orient hues, unborrow'd of the sun: 120
    Yet shall he mount, and keep his distant way
Beyond the limits of a vulgar fate,
Beneath the Good how far—but far above the Great.

THE BARD

A PINDARIC ODE

The following Ode is founded on a tradition current in Wales, that Edward the First, when he completed the conquest of that country, ordered all the Bards that fell into his hands to be put to death.—GRAY.

I. I.

"RUIN seize thee, ruthless King!
 Confusion on thy banners wait;
Tho' fann'd by Conquest's crimson wing,
 They mock the air with idle state.
Helm, nor hauberk's twisted mail,   5
Nor e'en thy virtues, Tyrant, shall avail
 To save thy secret soul from nightly fears,
 From Cambria's curse, from Cambria's tears!"
Such were the sounds that o'er the crested pride
 Of the first Edward scatter'd wild dismay,   10
As down the steep of Snowdon's shaggy side
 He wound with toilsome march his long array.
Stout Glo'ster stood aghast in speechless trance:
"To arms!" cried Mortimer, and couch'd his quiv'ring
  lance.

I. 2.

On a rock whose haughty brow   15
Frowns o'er old Conway's foaming flood,
 Robed in the sable garb of woe,
With haggard eyes the Poet stood;
(Loose his beard, and hoary hair
Stream'd, like a meteor, to the troubled air)   20
And with a master's hand, and prophet's fire,
Struck the deep sorrows of his lyre.

"Hark, how each giant-oak, and desert cave,
Sighs to the torrent's awful voice beneath!
O'er thee, oh King! their hundred arms they wave,   25
    Revenge on thee in hoarser murmurs breathe;
Vocal no more, since Cambria's fatal day,
To high-born Hoel's harp, or soft Llewellyn's lay.

I. 3.

"Cold is Cadwallo's tongue,
    That hush'd the stormy main: 30
Brave Urien sleeps upon his craggy bed:
    Mountains, ye mourn in vain
    Modred, whose magic song
Made huge Plinlimmon bow his cloud-topt head.
    On dreary Arvon's shore they lie,   35
Smear'd with gore, and ghastly pale:
Far, far aloof th' affrighted ravens sail;
    The famish'd eagle screams, and passes by.
Dear lost companions of my tuneful art,
    Dear as the light that visits these sad eyes,   40
Dear as the ruddy drops that warm my heart,
    Ye died amidst your dying country's cries—
No more I weep.   They do not sleep.
    On yonder cliffs, a grisly band,
I see them sit, they linger yet,   45
    Avengers of their native land:
With me in dreadful harmony they join,
And weave with bloody hands the tissue of thy line.

II. 1.

" 'Weave the warp, and weave the woof,
The winding sheet of Edward's race.   50

Give ample room, and verge enough
The characters of hell to trace.
Mark the year, and mark the night,
When Severn shall re-echo with affright
The shrieks of death, thro' Berkley's roof that ring,   55
Shrieks of an agonizing king!
   She-wolf of France, with unrelenting fangs,
That tear'st the bowels of thy mangled mate,
   From thee be born, who o'er thy country hangs
The scourge of heav'n. What terrors round him wait!   60
Amazement in his van, with flight combin'd,
And Sorrow's faded form, and Solitude behind.

II. 2.

   " 'Mighty victor, mighty lord!
Low on his funeral couch he lies!
   No pitying heart, no eye, afford   65
A tear to grace his obsequies.
   Is the sable warrior fled?
Thy son is gone. He rests among the dead.
The swarm, that in thy noontide beam were born?
Gone to salute the rising Morn.   70
Fair laughs the Morn, and soft the Zephyr blows,
   While proudly riding o'er the azure realm
In gallant trim the gilded vessel goes;
   Youth on the prow, and Pleasure at the helm;
Regardless of the sweeping Whirlwind's sway,   75
That, hush'd in grim repose, expects his evening prey.

II. 3.

   " 'Fill high the sparkling bowl,
The rich repast prepare,

Reft of a crown, he yet may share the feast:
Close by the regal chair　　　　　　　　　　80
　　Fell Thirst and Famine scowl
　　A baleful smile upon their baffled guest.
Heard ye the din of battle bray,
　　Lance to lance, and horse to horse?
　　Long years of havoc urge their destined course,　　85
And thro' the kindred squadrons mow their way.
　　Ye tower of Julius, London's lasting shame,
With many a foul and midnight murther fed,
　　Revere his consort's faith, his father's fame,
And spare the meek usurper's holy head.　　　　90
　　Above, below, the rose of snow,
　　Twin'd with her blushing foe, we spread:
The bristled boar in infant-gore
　　Wallows beneath the thorny shade.
Now, brothers, bending o'er the accursed loom,　　95
Stamp we our vengeance deep, and ratify his doom.

III. I.

" 'Edward, lo! to sudden fate
(Weave we the woof.　The thread is spun.)
　　Half of thy heart we consecrate.
(The web is wove.　The work is done.)'　　　　100
Stay, oh stay! nor thus forlorn
Leave me unbless'd, unpitied, here to mourn:
In yon bright track, that fires the western skies,
They melt, they vanish from my eyes.
But oh! what solemn scenes on Snowdon's height　　105
　　Descending slow their glitt'ring skirts unroll?
Visions of glory, spare my aching sight!
　　Ye unborn ages, crowd not on my soul'

No more our long-lost Arthur we bewail.
All hail, ye genuine kings, Britannia's issue, hail!   110

III. 2.

"Girt with many a baron bold
Sublime their starry fronts they rear;
    And gorgeous dames, and statesmen old
In bearded majesty, appear.
In the midst a form divine!   115
Her eye proclaims her of the Briton-line;
Her lion-port, her awe-commanding face,
Attemper'd sweet to virgin-grace.
What strings symphonious tremble in the air,
    What strains of vocal transport round her play   120
Hear from the grave, great Taliessin, hear;
    They breathe a soul to animate thy clay.
Bright Rapture calls, and soaring, as she sings,
Waves in the eye of Heav'n her many-colour'd wings.

III. 3.

"The verse adorn again   125
    Fierce War, and faithful Love,
And Truth severe, by fairy Fiction drest.
    In buskin'd measures move
Pale Grief, and pleasing Pain,
With Horror, tyrant of the throbbing breast.   130
    A voice, as of the cherub-choir,
Gales from blooming Eden bear;
And distant warblings lessen on my ear,
    That lost in long futurity expire.
Fond impious man, think'st thou yon sanguine cloud,   135
    Rais'd by thy breath, has quench'd the orb of day?

To-morrow he repairs the golden flood,
  And warms the nations with redoubled ray.
Enough for me; with joy I see
  The different doom our fates assign.   140
Be thine Despair, and sceptred Care;
  To triumph, and to die, are mine."
He spoke, and headlong from the mountain's height
Deep in the roaring tide he plung'd to endless night.

OLIVER GOLDSMITH

THE DESERTED VILLAGE AND OTHER
POEMS

THE DESERTED VILLAGE

DEDICATION

TO SIR JOSHUA REYNOLDS

DEAR SIR,—I can have no expectations, in an address of this kind, either to add to your reputation, or to establish my own. You can gain nothing from my admiration, as I am ignorant of that art in which you are said to excel; and I may lose much by the severity of your judgment, as few have a juster taste in poetry than you. Setting interest, therefore, aside, to which I never paid much attention, I must be indulged at present in following my affections. The only dedication I ever made was to my brother, because I loved him better than most other men. He is since dead. Permit me to ascribe this poem to you.

How far you may be pleased with the versification and mere mechanical parts of this attempt, I do not pretend to inquire; but I know you will object (and indeed several of our best and wisest friends concur in the opinion), that the depopulation it deplores is nowhere to be seen, and the disorders it laments are only to be found in the poet's own imagination. To this I can scarce make any other answer than that I sincerely believe what I have written; that I have taken all possible pains, in my country excursions, for these four or five years past, to be certain of what I allege; and that all my views and inquiries have led me to believe those miseries real, which I here attempt to display. But this is not the place to enter into an inquiry, whether the country be depopulating or not; the discussion would take up much room, and I should prove myself, at best, an indifferent politician, to tire the reader with a long preface, when I want his unfatigued attention to a long poem.

In regretting the depopulation of the country, I inveigh against the increase of our luxuries; and here also I expect the shout of modern politicians against me. For twenty or thirty years past, it has been the fashion to consider luxury as one of the greatest national advantages; and all the wisdom of antiquity, in that particular, as erroneous. Still, however, I must remain a professed ancient on that head, and continue to think those luxuries prejudicial to states by which so many vices are introduced, and so many kingdoms have been undone. Indeed, so much has been poured out of late on the other side of the question, that, merely for the sake of novelty and variety, one would sometimes wish to be in the right.—I am, dear Sir,

Your sincere Friend and ardent Admirer,

OLIVER GOLDSMITH.

THE DESERTED VILLAGE

Sweet Auburn! loveliest village of the plain,
Where health and plenty cheer'd the labouring swain,
Where smiling spring its earliest visit paid,
And parting summer's lingering blooms delay'd;
Dear lovely bowers of innocence and ease,   5
Seats of my youth, when every sport could please,
How often have I loiter'd o'er thy green,
Where humble happiness endear'd each scene!
How often have I paus'd on every charm,
The shelter'd cot, the cultivated farm,   10
The never-failing brook, the busy mill,
The decent church that topt the neighboring hill,
The hawthorn bush with seats beneath the shade,
For talking age and whispering lovers made!
How often have I blest the coming day,   15
When toil remitting lent its turn to play,
And all the village train, from labour free,
Led up their sports beneath the spreading tree;
While many a pastime circled in the shade,
The young contending as the old survey'd;   20
And many a gambol frolick'd o'er the ground,
And sleights of art and feats of strength went round!
And still, as each repeated pleasure tir'd,
Succeeding sports the mirthful band inspir'd;
The dancing pair that simply sought renown,   25
By holding out, to tire each other down;
The swain mistrustless of his smutted face,
While secret laughter titter'd round the place;

The bashful virgin's sidelong looks of love,
The matron's glance that would those looks reprove.   30
These were thy charms, sweet village! sports like these,
With sweet succession, taught even toil to please;
These round thy bowers their cheerful influence shed,
These were thy charms,—but all these charms are fled.

Sweet smiling village, loveliest of the lawn!   35
Thy sports are fled, and all thy charms withdrawn;
Amidst thy bowers the tyrant's hand is seen,
And desolation saddens all thy green:
One only master grasps the whole domain,
And half a tillage stints thy smiling plain.   40
No more thy glassy brook reflects the day,
But chok'd with sedges works its weedy way;
Along thy glades, a solitary guest,
The hollow-sounding bittern guards its nest;
Amidst thy desert-walks the lapwing flies,   45
And tires their echoes with unvaried cries.
Sunk are thy bowers in shapeless ruin all,
And the long grass o'ertops the mouldering wall;
And, trembling, shrinking from the spoiler's hand
Far, far away thy children leave the land.   50

Ill fares the land, to hastening ills a prey,
Where wealth accumulates, and men decay:
Princes and lords may flourish, or may fade—
A breath can make them, as a breath has made;
But a bold peasantry, their country's pride,   55
When once destroy'd, can never be supplied.

A time there was, ere England's griefs began,
When every rood of ground maintain'd its man;

For him light labour spread her wholesome store,
Just gave what life requir'd, but gave no more;   60
His best companions, innocence and health;
And his best riches, ignorance of wealth.

But times are alter'd; trade's unfeeling train
Usurp the land, and dispossess the swain;
Along the lawn, where scatter'd hamlets rose,   65
Unwieldy wealth and cumbrous pomp repose;
And every want to opulence allied,
And every pang that folly pays to pride.
Those gentle hours that plenty bade to bloom,
Those calm desires that ask'd but little room,   70
Those healthful sports that grac'd the peaceful scene,
Liv'd in each look, and brighten'd all the green:
These, far departing, seek a kinder shore,
And rural mirth and manners are no more.

Sweet Auburn! parent of the blissful hour,   75
Thy glades forlorn confess the tyrant's power.
Here, as I take my solitary rounds
Amidst thy tangling walks and ruin'd grounds,
And, many a year elaps'd, return to view
Where once the cottage stood, the hawthorn grew,   80
Remembrance wakes, with all her busy train,
Swells at my breast, and turns the past to pain.

In all my wanderings round this world of care,
In all my griefs—and God has given my share—
I still had hopes, my latest hours to crown,   85
Amidst these humble bowers to lay me down;
To husband out life's taper at the close,
And keep the flame from wasting by repose;

I still had hopes—for pride attends us still—
Amidst the swains to show my book-learn'd skill,   90
Around my fire an evening group to draw,
And tell of all I felt, and all I saw;
And, as a hare, whom hounds and horns pursue,
Pants to the place from whence at first she flew,
I still had hopes, my long vexations past,   95
Here to return,—and die at home at last.

O blest retirement! friend to life's decline,
Retreat from care, that never must be mine,
How happy he who crowns in shades like these
A youth of labour with an age of ease;   100
Who quits a world where strong temptations try,
And, since 't is hard to combat, learns to fly!
For him no wretches, born to work and weep,
Explore the mine, or tempt the dangerous deep:
No surly porter stands in guilty state,   105
To spurn imploring famine from the gate:
But on he moves to meet his latter end,
Angels around befriending virtue's friend;
Bends to the grave with unperceiv'd decay,
While resignation gently slopes the way;   110
And, all his prospects brightening to the last,
His heaven commences ere the world be past.

Sweet was the sound, when oft at evening's close
Up yonder hill the village murmur rose.
There, as I pass'd with careless steps and slow,   115
The mingling notes came soften'd from below:
The swain responsive as the milkmaid sung,
The sober herd that low'd to meet their young;
The noisy geese that gabbled o'er the pool;

The playful children just let loose from school;   120
The watch-dog's voice that bay'd the whispering wind,
And the loud laugh that spoke the vacant mind:
These all in sweet confusion sought the shade,
And fill'd each pause the nightingale had made.
But now the sounds of population fail,   125
No cheerful murmurs fluctuate in the gale,
No busy steps the grass-grown footway tread,
For all the bloomy flush of life is fled—
All but yon widow'd, solitary thing
That feebly bends beside the plashy spring;   130
She, wretched matron,—forc'd in age, for bread,
To strip the brook with mantling cresses spread,
To pick her wintry fagot from the thorn,
To seek her nightly shed, and weep till morn—
She only left of all the harmless train,   135
The sad historian of the pensive plain.

Near yonder copse, where once the garden smil'd,
And still where many a garden flower grows wild,
There, where a few torn shrubs the place disclose,
The village preacher's modest mansion rose.   140
A man he was to all the country dear,
And passing rich with forty pounds a year.
Remote from towns he ran his godly race,
Nor e'er had chang'd, nor wish'd to change, his place;
Unpractis'd he to fawn, or seek for power,   145
By doctrines fashion'd to the varying hour;
Far other aims his heart had learn'd to prize,
More skill'd to raise the wretched than to rise.
His house was known to all the vagrant train,
He chid their wanderings, but reliev'd their pain;   150
The long-remember'd beggar was his guest,

Whose beard descending swept his aged breast;
The ruin'd spendthrift, now no longer proud,
Claim'd kindred there, and had his claims allow'd.
The broken soldier, kindly bade to stay,　　　155
Sate by his fire, and talk'd the night away;
Wept o'er his wounds, or, tales of sorrow done,
Shoulder'd his crutch, and show'd how fields were won.
Pleas'd with his guests, the good man learn'd to glow,
And quite forgot their vices in their woe;　　　160
Careless their merits or their faults to scan,
His pity gave ere charity began.

Thus to relieve the wretched was his pride,
And e'en his failings lean'd to virtue's side;
But in his duty prompt at every call,　　　165
He watch'd and wept, he pray'd and felt for all;
And as a bird each fond endearment tries
To tempt its new-fledg'd offspring to the skies,
He tried each art, reprov'd each dull delay,
Allur'd to brighter worlds, and led the way.　　　170

Beside the bed where parting life was laid,
And sorrow, guilt, and pain, by turns dismay'd,
The reverend champion stood. At his control,
Despair and anguish fled the struggling soul;
Comfort came down the trembling wretch to raise,　　　175
And his last faltering accents whisper'd praise.

At church, with meek and unaffected grace,
His looks adorn'd the venerable place;
Truth from his lips prevail'd with double sway,
And fools, who came to scoff, remain'd to pray.　　　180
The service past, around the pious man,

With steady zeal, each honest rustic ran;
Even children follow'd, with endearing wile,
And pluck'd his gown, to share the good man's smile.
His ready smile a parent's warmth exprest,   185
Their welfare pleas'd him, and their cares distrest;
To them his heart, his love, his griefs, were given,
But all his serious thoughts had rest in heaven:
As some tall cliff that lifts its awful form,
Swells from the vale, and midway leaves the storm,   190
Though round its breast the rolling clouds are spread,
Eternal sunshine settles on its head.

    Beside yon straggling fence that skirts the way
With blossom'd furze unprofitably gay,
There, in his noisy mansion, skill'd to rule,   195
The village master taught his little school.
A man severe he was, and stern to view;
I knew him well, and every truant knew:
Well had the boding tremblers learn'd to trace
The day's disasters in his morning face;   200
Full well they laugh'd, with counterfeited glee,
At all his jokes, for many a joke had he:
Full well the busy whisper, circling round,
Convey'd the dismal tidings when he frown'd.
Yet he was kind, or, if severe in aught,   205
The love he bore to learning was in fault.
The village all declar'd how much he knew;
'T was certain he could write, and cipher too;
Lands he could measure, terms and tides presage,
And even the story ran—that he could gauge;   210
In arguing, too, the parson own'd his skill,
For even though vanquish'd he could argue still;
While words of learned length and thundering sound

Amaz'd the gazing rustics rang'd around;
And still they gaz'd, and still the wonder grew   215
That one small head could carry all he knew.

But past is all his fame.   The very spot
Where many a time he triumph'd is forgot.
Near yonder thorn, that lifts its head on high,
Where once the sign-post caught the passing eye,   220
Low lies that house where nut-brown draughts inspir'd,
Where gray-beard mirth and smiling toil retir'd,
Where village statesmen talk'd with looks profound,
And news much older than their ale went round.
Imagination fondly stoops to trace   225
The parlour splendours of that festive place:
The whitewash'd wall, the nicely sanded floor,
The varnish'd clock that click'd behind the door;
The chest contriv'd a double debt to pay—
A bed by night, a chest of drawers by day;   230
The pictures plac'd for ornament and use,
The twelve good rules, the royal game of goose;
The hearth, except when winter chill'd the day,
With aspen boughs, and flowers, and fennel gay,
While broken teacups, wisely kept for show,   235
Rang'd o'er the chimney, glisten'd in a row.

Vain, transitory splendours! could not all
Reprieve the tottering mansion from its fall?
Obscure it sinks, nor shall it more impart
An hour's importance to the poor man's heart.   240
Thither no more the peasant shall repair
To sweet oblivion of his daily care;
No more the farmer's news, the barber's tale,
No more the woodman's ballad shall prevail;

No more the smith his dusky brow shall clear, 245
Relax his ponderous strength, and lean to hear;
The host himself no longer shall be found
Careful to see the mantling bliss go round;
Nor the coy maid, half willing to be prest,
Shall kiss the cup to pass it to the rest. 250

Yes! let the rich deride, the proud disdain,
These simple blessings of the lowly train;
To me more dear, congenial to my heart,
One native charm, than all the gloss of art:
Spontaneous joys, where nature has its play, 255
The soul adopts, and owns their first-born sway;
Lightly they frolic o'er the vacant mind,
Unenvied, unmolested, unconfin'd.
But the long pomp, the midnight masquerade,
With all the freaks of wanton wealth array'd,— 260
In these, ere triflers half their wish obtain,
The toiling pleasure sickens into pain;
And even while fashion's brightest arts decoy,
The heart distrusting asks, if this be joy.

Ye friends to truth, ye statesmen, who survey 265
The rich man's joys increase, the poor's decay,
'T is yours to judge how wide the limits stand
Between a splendid and a happy land.
Proud swells the tide with loads of freighted ore,
And shouting Folly hails them from her shore; 270
Hoards e'en beyond the miser's wish abound,
And rich men flock from all the world around.
Yet count our gains. This wealth is but a name,
That leaves our useful products still the same.
Not so the loss. The man of wealth and pride 275
Takes up a space that many poor supplied;

Space for his lake, his park's extended bounds,
Space for his horses, equipage, and hounds:
The robe that wraps his limbs in silken sloth
Has robb'd the neighbouring fields of half their growth; 280
His seat, where solitary sports are seen,
Indignant spurns the cottage from the green;
Around the world each needful product flies,
For all the luxuries the world supplies.
While thus the land, adorn'd for pleasure, all   285
In barren splendour feebly waits the fall.

As some fair female, unadorn'd and plain,
Secure to please while youth confirms her reign,
Slights every borrow'd charm that dress supplies,
Nor shares with art the triumph of her eyes; -   290
But when those charms are past, for charms are frail,
When time advances, and when lovers fail,
She then shines forth, solicitous to bless,
In all the glaring impotence of dress:
Thus fares the land, by luxury betray'd;   295
In nature's simplest charms at first array'd,
But, verging to decline, its splendours rise,
Its vistas strike, its palaces surprise;
While, scourged by famine from the smiling land,
The mournful peasant leads his humble band;   300
And while he sinks, without one arm to save,
The country blooms—a garden and a grave.

Where then, ah! where shall poverty reside,
To 'scape the pressure of contiguous pride?
If to some common's fenceless limits stray'd,   305
He drives his flock to pick the scanty blade,
Those fenceless fields the sons of wealth divide,
And even the bare-worn common is denied.

If to the city sped, what waits him there?
To see profusion that he must not share;   310
To see ten thousand baneful arts combin'd,
To pamper luxury, and thin mankind;
To see those joys the sons of pleasure know
Extorted from his fellow-creature's woe.
Here, while the courtier glitters in brocade,   315
There the pale artist plies the sickly trade;
Here, while the proud their long-drawn pomps display,
There the black gibbet glooms beside the way.
The dome where Pleasure holds her midnight reign,
Here, richly deck'd, admits the gorgeous train;   320
Tumultuous grandeur crowds the blazing square,
The rattling chariots clash, the torches glare.
Sure scenes like these no troubles e'er annoy!
Sure these denote one universal joy!
Are these thy serious thoughts? Ah! turn thine eyes 325
Where the poor houseless shivering female lies.
She once, perhaps, in village plenty blest,
Has wept at tales of innocence distrest;
Her modest looks the cottage might adorn,
Sweet as the primrose peeps beneath the thorn;   330
Now lost to all, her friends, her virtue fled,
Near her betrayer's door she lays her head,
And, pinch'd with cold, and shrinking from the shower,
With heavy heart deplores that luckless hour,
When idly first, ambitious of the town,   335
She left her wheel, and robes of country brown.

    Do thine, sweet Auburn, thine, the loveliest train,
Do thy fair tribes participate her pain?
Even now, perhaps, by cold and hunger led,
At proud men's doors they ask a little bread.   340

Ah, no! To distant climes, a dreary scene,
Where half the convex world intrudes between,
Through torrid tracts with fainting steps they go,
Where wild Altama murmurs to their woe.
Far different there from all that charm'd before,   345
The various terrors of that horrid shore:
Those blazing suns that dart a downward ray,
And fiercely shed intolerable day;
Those matted woods where birds forget to sing,
But silent bats in drowsy clusters cling;   350
Those pois'nous fields with rank luxuriance crown'd
Where the dark scorpion gathers death around;
Where at each step the stranger fears to wake
The rattling terrors of the vengeful snake;
Where crouching tigers wait their hapless prey   355
And savage men more murderous still than they;
While oft in whirls the mad tornado flies,
Mingling the ravag'd landscape with the skies.
Far different these from every former scene,
The cooling brook, the grassy-vested green,   360
The breezy covert of the warbling grove,
That only shelter'd thefts of harmless love.

Good Heaven! what sorrows gloom'd that parting day
That call'd them from their native walks away;
When the poor exiles, every pleasure past,   365
Hung round the bowers, and fondly look'd their last,
And took a long farewell, and wish'd in vain
For seats like these beyond the western main;
And, shuddering still to face the distant deep,
Return'd and wept, and still return'd to weep!   370
The good old sire, the first prepar'd to go
To new-found worlds, and wept for others' woe;

But for himself, in conscious virtue brave,
He only wish'd for worlds beyond the grave.
His lovely daughter, lovelier in her tears, 375
The fond companion of his helpless years,
Silent went next, neglectful of her charms,
And left a lover's for a father's arms.
With louder plaints the mother spoke her woes,
And bless'd the cot where every pleasure rose; 380
And kiss'd her thoughtless babes with many a tear
And clasp'd them close, in sorrow doubly dear;
Whilst her fond husband strove to lend relief
In all the silent manliness of grief.

O Luxury! thou curst by Heaven's decree, 385
How ill exchang'd are things like these for thee!
How do thy potions, with insidious joy,
Diffuse their pleasures only to destroy!
Kingdoms by thee, to sickly greatness grown,
Boast of a florid vigour not their own: 390
At every draught more large and large they grow,
A bloated mass of rank, unwieldy woe;
Till sapp'd their strength, and every part unsound,
Down, down they sink, and spread a ruin round.

Even now the devastation is begun, 395
And half the business of destruction done;
Even now, methinks, as pondering here I stand,
I see the rural Virtues leave the land.
Down where yon anchoring vessel spreads the sail,
That idly waiting flaps with every gale, 400
Downward they move, a melancholy band,
Pass from the shore, and darken all the strand.
Contented Toil, and hospitable Care,

And kind connubial Tenderness, are there;
And Piety with wishes plac'd above,   405
And steady Loyalty, and faithful Love.
And thou, sweet Poetry, thou loveliest maid,
Still first to fly where sensual joys invade;
Unfit, in these degenerate times of shame,
To catch the heart, or strike for honest fame;   410
Dear charming nymph, neglected and decried,
My shame in crowds, my solitary pride;
Thou source of all my bliss and all my woe,
That found'st me poor at first, and keep'st me so;
Thou guide, by which the nobler arts excel,   415
Thou nurse of every virtue, fare thee well!
Farewell! and oh! where'er thy voice be tried,
On Torno's cliffs, or Pambamarca's side,
Whether where equinoctial fervours glow,
Or winter wraps the polar world in snow,   420
Still let thy voice, prevailing over time,
Redress the rigours of the inclement clime;
Aid slighted truth with thy persuasive strain;
Teach erring man to spurn the rage of gain;
Teach him, that states of native strength possest,   425
Though very poor, may still be very blest;
That trade's proud empire hastes to swift decay,
As ocean sweeps the labour'd mole away;
While self-dependent power can time defy,
As rocks resist the billows and the sky.   430

THE TRAVELLER

DEDICATION

TO THE REV. HENRY GOLDSMITH

DEAR SIR,—I am sensible that the friendship between us can acquire no new force from the ceremonies of a dedication; and perhaps it demands an excuse thus to prefix your name to my attempts, which you decline giving with your own. But as a part of this poem was formerly written to you from Switzerland, the whole can now, with propriety, be only inscribed to you. It will also throw a light upon many parts of it, when the reader understands that it is addressed to a man who, despising fame and fortune, has retired early to happiness and obscurity, with an income of forty pounds a year.

I now perceive, my dear brother, the wisdom of your humble choice. You have entered upon a sacred office, where the harvest is great, and the labourers are but few; while you have left the field of ambition, where the labourers are many, and the harvest not worth carrying away. But of all kinds of ambition,—what from the refinement of the times, from different systems of criticism, and from the divisions of party,—that which pursues poetical fame is the widest.

Poetry makes a principal amusement among unpolished nations; but in a country verging to the extremes of refinement, painting and music come in for a share. As these offer the feeble mind a less laborious entertainment, they at first rival poetry, and at length supplant her: they engross all that favour once shown to her, and, though but younger sisters, seize upon the elder's birthright.

Yet, however this art may be neglected by the powerful, it is still in greater danger from the mistaken efforts of the learned to improve it. What criticisms have we not heard of late in favour of blank verse and Pindaric odes, choruses, anapests and iambics, alliterative care and happy negligence! Every absurdity has now a champion to defend it; and as he is generally much in the wrong, so he has always much to say; for error is ever talkative.

But there is an enemy to this art still more dangerous —I mean party. Party entirely distorts the judgment, and destroys the taste. When the mind is once infected with this disease, it can only find pleasure in what contributes to increase the distemper. Like the tiger, that seldom desists from pursuing man after having once preyed upon human flesh, the reader, who has once gratified his appetite with calumny, makes, ever after, the most agreeable feast upon murdered reputation. Such readers generally admire some half-witted thing, who wants to be thought a bold man,[1] having lost the character of a wise one. Him they dignify with the name of poet: his tawdry lampoons are called satires; his turbulence is said to be force, and his frenzy fire.

What reception a poem may find, which has neither abuse, party, nor blank verse to support it, I cannot tell, nor am I solicitous to know. My aims are right. With-

---

[1] Churchill, at whom all this is aimed, died 4th November, 1764, while the first edition of "The Traveller" was passing through the press.—PETER CUNNINGHAM.

out espousing the cause of any party, I have attempted to moderate the rage of all. I have endeavoured to show, that there may be equal happiness in states that are differently governed from our own; that every state has a particular principle of happiness, and that this principle in each may be carried to a mischievous excess. There are few can judge, better than yourself, how far these positions are illustrated in this poem. I am, dear Sir,

Your most affectionate Brother,

OLIVER GOLDSMITH.

THE TRAVELLER;

OR,

A PROSPECT OF SOCIETY

REMOTE, unfriended, melancholy, slow,—
Or by the lazy Scheldt or wandering Po;
Or onward, where the rude Carinthian boor
Against the houseless stranger shuts the door;
Or where Campania's plain forsaken lies,   5
A weary waste expanding to the skies;—
Where'er I roam, whatever realms to see,
My heart untravell'd fondly turns to thee;
Still to my brother turns, with ceaseless pain,
And drags at each remove a lengthening chain.   10

   Eternal blessings crown my earliest friend,
And round his dwelling guardian saints attend:
Blest be that spot, where cheerful guests retire
To pause from toil, and trim their evening fire;
Blest that abode, where want and pain repair,   15
And every stranger finds a ready chair;
Blest be those feasts with simple plenty crown'd,
Where all the ruddy family around
Laugh at the jests or pranks that never fail,
Or sigh with pity at some mournful tale,   20
Or press the bashful stranger to his food,
And learn the luxury of doing good.

But me, not destin'd such delights to share,
My prime of life in wandering spent and care—
Impell'd, with steps unceasing, to pursue   25
Some fleeting good, that mocks me with the view;
That, like the circle bounding earth and skies,
Allures from far, yet, as I follow, flies; —
My fortune leads to traverse realms alone,
And find no spot of all the world my own.   30
Ev'n now, where Alpine solitudes ascend,
I sit me down a pensive hour to spend;
And, plac'd on high above the storm's career,
Look downward where an hundred realms appear:
Lakes, forests, cities, plains, extending wide,   35
The pomp of kings, the shepherd's humbler pride.

When thus creation's charms around combine,
Amidst the store, should thankless pride repine?
Say, should the philosophic mind disdain
That good which makes each humbler bosom vain?   40
Let school-taught pride dissemble all it can,
These little things are great to little man;
And wiser he, whose sympathetic mind
Exults in all the good of all mankind.
Ye glittering towns, with wealth and splendour crown'd, 45
Ye fields, where summer spreads profusion round,
Ye lakes, whose vessels catch the busy gale,
Ye bending swains, that dress the flowery vale;
For me your tributary stores combine:
Creation's heir, the world—the world is mine!   50

As some lone miser, visiting his store,
Bends at his treasure, counts, recounts it o'er:
Hoards after hoards his rising raptures fill,

Yet still he sighs, for hoards are wanting still:
Thus to my breast alternate passions rise,   55
Pleas'd with each good that Heaven to man supplies:
Yet oft a sigh prevails, and sorrows fall,
To see the hoard of human bliss so small;
And oft I wish, amidst the scene, to find
Some spot to real happiness consign'd,   60
Where my worn soul, each wandering hope at rest,
May gather bliss to see my fellows blest.

But where to find that happiest spot below,
Who can direct, when all pretend to know?
The shuddering tenant of the frigid zone   65
Boldly proclaims that happiest spot his own;
Extols the treasures of his stormy seas,
And his long nights of revelry and ease;
The naked negro, panting at the line,
Boasts of his golden sands and palmy wine,   70
Basks in the glare, or stems the tepid wave,
And thanks his gods for all the good they gave.
Such is the patriot's boast, where'er we roam;
His first, best country ever is at home.
·And yet, perhaps, if countries we compare,   75
And estimate the blessings which they share,
Though patriots flatter, still shall wisdom find
An equal portion dealt to all mankind;
As different good, by art or nature given,
To different nations makes their blessings even.   80

Nature, a mother kind alike to all,
Still grants her bliss at labour's earnest call;
With food as well the peasant is supplied
On Idra's cliffs as Arno's shelvy side;

And, though the rocky-crested summits frown,   85
These rocks by custom turn to beds of down.
From art more various are the blessings sent:
Wealth, commerce, honour, liberty, content.
Yet these each other's power so strong contest,
That either seems destructive of the rest.   90
Where wealth and freedom reign, contentment fails
And honour sinks where commerce long prevails.
Hence every state, to one lov'd blessing prone,
Conforms and models life to that alone:
Each to the fav'rite happiness attends,   95
And spurns the plan that aims at other ends;
Till, carried to excess in each domain,
This fav'rite good begets peculiar pain.

But let us try these truths with closer eyes,
And trace them through the prospect as it lies.   100
Here for a while, my proper cares resign'd,
Here let me sit in sorrow for mankind;
Like yon neglected shrub, at random cast,
That shades the steep, and sighs at every blast.

Far to the right, where Apennine ascends,   105
Bright as the summer, Italy extends;
Its uplands sloping deck the mountain's side,
Woods over woods in gay theatric pride;
While oft some temple's mould'ring tops between
With venerable grandeur mark the scene.   110

Could nature's bounty satisfy the breast,
The sons of Italy were surely blest.
Whatever fruits in different climes are found,
That proudly rise, or humbly court the ground;
Whatever blooms in torrid tracts appear,   115
Whose bright succession decks the varied year;

Whatever sweets salute the northern sky
With vernal lives, that blossom but to die:
These, here disporting, own the kindred soil,
Nor ask luxuriance from the planter's toil;   120
While sea-born gales their gelid wings expand
To winnow fragrance round the smiling land.

But small the bliss that sense alone bestows,
And sensual bliss is all the nation knows.
In florid beauty groves and fields appear,   125
Man seems the only growth that dwindles here.
Contrasted faults through all his manners reign:
Though poor, luxurious; though submissive, vain;
Though grave, yet trifling; zealous, yet untrue;
And even in penance planning sins anew.   130
All evils here contaminate the mind,
That opulence departed leaves behind.
For wealth was theirs; not far remov'd the date,
When commerce proudly flourished through the state.
At her command the palace learnt to rise,   135
Again the long-fall'n column sought the skies;
The canvas glow'd beyond ev'n nature warm,
The pregnant quarry teem'd with human form;
Till, more unsteady than the southern gale,
Commerce on other shores display'd her sail;   140
While nought remain'd of all that riches gave,
But towns unmann'd, and lords without a slave:
And late the nation found, with fruitless skill,
Its former strength was but plethoric ill.

Yet still the loss of wealth is here supplied   145
By arts, the splendid wrecks of former pride;
From these the feeble heart and long-fallen mind
An easy compensation seem to find.

Here may be seen, in bloodless pomp array'd,
The pasteboard triumph and the cavalcade;   150
Processions form'd for piety and love,
A mistress or a saint in every grove.
By sports like these are all their cares beguil'd,
The sports of children satisfy the child;
Each nobler aim, represt by long control,   155
Now sinks at last, or feebly mans the soul;
While low delights, succeeding fast behind,
In happier meanness occupy the mind.
As in those domes where Cæsars once bore sway,
Defac'd by time and tott'ring in decay,   160
There in the ruin, heedless of the dead,
The shelter-seeking peasant builds his shed;
And, wondering man could want the larger pile,
Exults, and owns his cottage with a smile.

My soul, turn from them; turn we to survey   165
Where rougher climes a nobler race display;
Where the bleak Swiss their stormy mansion tread,
And force a churlish soil for scanty bread.
No product here the barren hills afford,
But man and steel, the soldier and his sword;   170
No vernal blooms their torpid rocks array,
But winter lingering chills the lap of May;
No zephyr fondly sues the mountain's breast,
But meteors glare, and stormy glooms invest.

Yet still, even here, content can spread a charm,   175
Redress the clime, and all its rage disarm.
Though poor the peasant's hut, his feasts though small,
He sees his little lot the lot of all;
Sees no contiguous palace rear its head
To shame the meanness of his humble shed;   180

No costly lord the sumptuous banquet deal
To make him loathe his vegetable meal;
But calm, and bred in ignorance and toil,
Each wish contracting, fits him to the soil.
Cheerful, at morn, he wakes from short repose,   185
Breasts the keen air, and carols as he goes;
With patient angle trolls the finny deep,
Or drives his venturous ploughshare to the steep;
Or seeks the den where snow-tracks mark the way,
And drags the struggling savage into day.   190
At night returning, every labour sped,
He sits him down, the monarch of a shed;
Smiles by his cheerful fire, and round surveys
His children's looks, that brighten at the blaze;
While his lov'd partner, boastful of her hoard,   195
Displays her cleanly platter on the board;
And haply too some pilgrim, thither led,
With many a tale repays the nightly bed.

Thus every good his native wilds impart,
Imprints the patriot passion on his heart;   200
And ev'n those hills that round his mansion rise
Enhance the bliss his scanty fund supplies.
Dear is that shed to which his soul conforms,
And dear that hill which lifts him to the storms:
And as a child, when scaring sounds molest,   205
Clings close and closer to the mother's breast,
So the loud torrent and the whirlwind's roar
But bind him to his native mountains more.

Such are the charms to barren states assign'd;
Their wants but few, their wishes all confin'd.   210
Yet let them only share the praises due;
If few their wants, their pleasures are but few;

For every want that stimulates the breast
Becomes a source of pleasure when redrest.
Whence from such lands each pleasing science flies,   215
That first excites desire, and then supplies:
Unknown to them, when sensual pleasures cloy,
To fill the languid pause with finer joy;
Unknown those powers that raise the soul to flame,
Catch every nerve, and vibrate through the frame: 220
Their level life is but a smouldering fire,
Unquench'd by want, unfann'd by strong desire;
Unfit for raptures, or, if raptures cheer
On some high festival of once a year,
In wild excess the vulgar breast takes fire,   225
Till, buried in debauch, the bliss expire.

But not their joys alone thus coarsely flow;
Their morals, like their pleasures, are but low:
For, as refinement stops, from sire to son,
Unalter'd, unimprov'd, the manners run;   230
And love's and friendship's finely pointed dart
Fall blunted from each indurated heart.
Some sterner virtues o'er the mountain's breast
May sit, like falcons cowering on the nest;
But all the gentler morals, such as play   235
Through life's more cultur'd walks, and charm the way,—
These, far dispers'd, on timorous pinions fly,
To sport and flutter in a kinder sky.

To kinder skies, where gentler manners reign,
I turn; and France displays her bright domain.   240
Gay, sprightly land of mirth and social ease,
Pleas'd with thyself, whom all the world can please,
How often have I led thy sportive choir,

With tuneless pipe, beside the murmuring Loire!
Where shading elms along the margin grew,   245
And freshen'd from the wave the zephyr flew;
And haply, though my harsh touch, faltering still,
But mock'd all tune, and marr'd the dancer's skill,
Yet would the village praise my wondrous power,
And dance, forgetful of the noontide hour.   250
Alike all ages: dames of ancient days
Have led their children through the mirthful maze,
And the gay grandsire, skill'd in gestic lore,
Has frisk'd beneath the burthen of threescore.

So blest a life these thoughtless realms display;   255
Thus idly busy rolls their world away.
Theirs are those arts that mind to mind endear,
For honour forms the social temper here:
Honour, that praise which real merit gains,
Or even imaginary worth obtains,   260
Here passes current; paid from hand to hand,
It shifts in splendid traffic round the land;
From courts, to camps, to cottages it strays,
And all are taught an avarice of praise.
They please, are pleas'd; they give to get esteem,   265
Till, seeming blest, they grow to what they seem.

But while this softer art their bliss supplies,
It gives their follies also room to rise;
For praise too dearly lov'd, or warmly sought,
Enfeebles all internal strength of thought: 270
And the weak soul, within itself unblest,
Leans for all pleasure on another's breast.
Hence ostentation here, with tawdry art,
Pants for the vulgar praise which fools impart;

Here vanity assumes her pert grimace,   275
And trims her robes of frieze with copper lace;
Here beggar pride defrauds her daily cheer,
To boast one splendid banquet once a year:
The mind still turns where shifting fashion draws,
Nor weighs the solid worth of self-applause.   280

To men of other minds my fancy flies,
Embosom'd in the deep where Holland lies.
Methinks her patient sons before me stand,
Where the broad ocean leans against the land,
And, sedulous to stop the coming tide,   285
Lift the tall rampire's artificial pride.
Onward methinks, and diligently slow,
The firm connected bulwark seems to grow,
Spreads its long arms amidst the watery roar,
Scoops out an empire, and usurps the shore.   290
While the pent ocean, rising o'er the pile,
Sees an amphibious world beneath him smile:
The slow canal, the yellow-blossom'd vale,
The willow-tufted bank, the gliding sail,
The crowded mart, the cultivated plain,—   295
A new creation rescued from his reign.

Thus, while around the wave-subjected soil
Impels the native to repeated toil,
Industrious habits in each bosom reign,
And industry begets a love of gain.   300
Hence all the good from opulence that springs,
With all those ills superfluous treasure brings,
Are here display'd. Their much lov'd wealth imparts
Convenience, plenty, elegance, and arts;
But, view them closer, craft and fraud appear;   305

Even liberty itself is barter'd here.
At gold's superior charms all freedom flies;
The needy sell it, and the rich man buys.
A land of tyrants, and a den of slaves,
Here wretches seek dishonourable graves,   310
And calmly bent, to servitude conform,
Dull as their lakes that slumber in the storm.

Heavens! how unlike their Belgic sires of old—
Rough, poor, content, ungovernably bold;
War in each breast, and freedom on each brow;   315
How much unlike the sons of Britain now!

Fir'd at the sound, my genius spreads her wing,
And flies where Britain courts the western spring;
Where lawns extend that scorn Arcadian pride,
And brighter streams than fam'd Hydaspes glide.   320
There all around the gentlest breezes stray,
There gentle music melts on every spray;
Creation's mildest charms are there combin'd:
Extremes are only in the master's mind!
Stern o'er each bosom Reason holds her state,   325
With daring aims irregularly great;
Pride in their port, defiance in their eye,
I see the lords of human kind pass by;
Intent on high designs, a thoughtful band,
By forms unfashion'd, fresh from Nature's hand,   330
Fierce in their native hardiness of soul,
True to imagin'd right, above control;
While even the peasant boasts these rights to scan,
And learns to venerate himself as man.

Thine, Freedom, thine the blessings pictur'd here,   335
Thine are those charms that dazzle and endear;

Too blest, indeed, were such without alloy;
But, foster'd even by freedom, ills annoy.
That independence Britons prize too high
Keeps man from man, and breaks the social tie;   340
The self-dependent lordlings stand alone,
All claims that bind and sweeten life unknown.
Here, by the bonds of nature feebly held,
Minds combat minds, repelling and repell'd;
Ferments arise, imprison'd factions roar,   345
Represt ambition struggles round her shore;
Till, over-wrought, the general system feels
Its motions stop, or frenzy fire the wheels.

Nor this the worst.   As nature's ties decay,
As duty, love, and honour fail to sway,   350
Fictitious bonds, the bonds of wealth and law,
Still gather strength, and force unwilling awe.
Hence all obedience bows to these alone,
And talent sinks, and merit weeps unknown;
Till time may come, when, stript of all her charms,   355
The land of scholars, and the nurse of arms,
Where noble stems transmit the patriot flame,
Where kings have toil'd and poets wrote for fame,
One sink of level avarice shall lie,
And scholars, soldiers, kings, unhonour'd die.   360

Yet think not, thus when Freedom's ills I state,
I mean to flatter kings, or court the great:
Ye powers of truth, that bid my soul aspire,
Far from my bosom drive the low desire;
And thou, fair Freedom, taught alike to feel   365
The rabble's rage, and tyrant's angry steel;
Thou transitory flower, alike undone

By proud contempt, or favour's fostering sun,
Still may thy blooms the changeful clime endure!
I only would repress them to secure: 370
For just experience tells, in every soil,
That those who think must govern those that toil;
And all that Freedom's highest aims can reach,
Is but to lay proportion'd loads on each.
Hence, should one order disproportion'd grow,   375
Its double weight must ruin all below.

Oh, then how blind to all that truth requires,
Who think it freedom when a part aspires!
Calm is my soul, nor apt to rise in arms,
Except when fast approaching danger warms: 380
But when contending chiefs blockade the throne,
Contracting regal power to stretch their own;
When I behold a factious band agree
To call it freedom when themselves are free;
Each wanton judge new penal statutes draw,   385
Laws grind the poor, and rich men rule the law;
The wealth of climes, where savage nations roam,
Pillag'd from slaves to purchase slaves at home;
Fear, pity, justice, indignation, start,
Tear off reserve, and bare my swelling heart;   390
Till, half a patriot, half a coward grown,
I fly from petty tyrants to the throne.

Yes, Brother, curse with me that baleful hour,
When first ambition struck at regal power,
And thus polluting honour in its source,   395
Gave wealth to sway the mind with double force.
Have we not seen, round Britain's peopled shore,
Her useful sons exchang'd for useless ore?

Seen all her triumphs but destruction haste,
Like flaring tapers brightening as they waste;   400
Seen opulence, her grandeur to maintain,
Lead stern depopulation in her train,
And over fields where scatter'd hamlets rose,
In barren, solitary pomp repose?
Have we not seen, at pleasure's lordly call,   405
The smiling, long frequented village fall?
Beheld the duteous son, the sire decay'd,
The modest matron, and the blushing maid,
Forc'd from their homes, a melancholy train,
To traverse climes beyond the western main;   410
Where wild Oswego spreads her swamps around,
And Niagara stuns with thundering sound?

Even now, perhaps, as there some pilgrim strays
Through tangled forests, and through dangerous ways,
Where beasts with man divided empire claim,   415
And the brown Indian marks with murderous aim;
There, while above the giddy tempest flies,
And all around distressful yells arise,
The pensive exile, bending with his woe,
To stop too fearful, and too faint to go,   420
Casts a long look where England's glories shine,
And bids his bosom sympathise with mine.

Vain, very vain, my weary search to find
That bliss which only centres in the mind:
Why have I stray'd from pleasure and repose,   425
To seek a good each government bestows?
In every government, though terrors reign,
Though tyrant kings or tyrant laws restrain,
How small, of all that human hearts endure,

That part which laws or kings can cause or cure!   430
Still to ourselves in every place consign'd,
Our own felicity we make or find:
With secret course, which no loud storms annoy
Glides the smooth current of domestic joy.
The lifted axe, the agonising wheel,   435
Luke's iron crown, and Damiens' bed of steel,
To men remote from power but rarely known,
Leave reason, faith, and conscience, all our own.

RETALIATION

OF old, when Scarron his companions invited,
Each guest brought his dish, and the feast was united;
If our landlord supplies us with beef and with fish,
Let each guest bring himself, and he brings the best dish:
Our Dean shall be venison, just fresh from the plains;   5
Our Burke shall be tongue, with the garnish of brains;
Our Will shall be wildfowl, of excellent flavour,
And Dick with his pepper shall heighten the savour:
Our Cumberland's sweetbread its place shall obtain,
And Douglas is pudding, substantial and plain;   10
Our Garrick's a salad, for in him we see
Oil, vinegar, sugar, and saltness agree:
To make out the dinner, full certain I am
That Ridge is anchovy, and Reynolds is lamb;
That Hickey's a capon, and, by the same rule,   15
Magnanimous Goldsmith a gooseberry fool.

At a dinner so various, at such a repast,
Who'd not be a glutton, and stick to the last?
Here, waiter, more wine! let me sit while I'm able,
Till all my companions sink under the table;   20
Then, with chaos and blunders encircling my head,
Let me ponder, and tell what I think of the dead.

Here lies the good dean, reunited to earth,
Who mixt reason with pleasure, and wisdom with mirth:
If he had any faults, he has left us in doubt,   25
At least in six weeks I could not find 'em out;
Yet some have declar'd, and it can't be denied 'em,
That slyboots was cursedly cunning to hide 'em.

Here lies our good Edmund, whose genius was such,
We scarcely can praise it or blame it too much;   30
Who, born for the universe, narrow'd his mind,
And to party gave up what was meant for mankind;
Though fraught with all learning, yet straining his throat
To persuade Tommy Townshend to lend him a vote;
Who, too deep for his hearers, still went on refining,   35
And thought of convincing, while they thought of dining:
Though equal to all things, for all things unfit;
Too nice for a statesman, too proud for a wit;
For a patriot too cool, for a drudge disobedient,
And too fond of the right to pursue the expedient.   40
In short, 'twas his fate, unemploy'd or in place, sir,
To eat mutton cold, and cut blocks with a razor.

Here lies honest William, whose heart was a mint,
While the owner ne'er knew half the good that was in 't;
The pupil of impulse, it forc'd him along,   45
His conduct still right, with his argument wrong.

Still aiming at honour, yet fearing to roam,
The coachman was tipsy, the chariot drove home:
Would you ask for his merits? alas! he had none;
What was good was spontaneous, his faults were his own. 50

Here lies honest Richard, whose fate I must sigh at;
Alas that such frolic should now be so quiet!
What spirits were his! what wit and what whim,
Now breaking a jest, and now breaking a limb;
Now wrangling and grumbling to keep up the ball,   55
Now teasing and vexing, yet laughing at all!
In short so provoking a devil was Dick,
That we wish'd him full ten times a day at Old Nick;
But, missing his mirth and agreeable vein,
As often we wish'd to have Dick back again.   60

Here Cumberland lies, having acted his parts,
The Terence of England, the mender of hearts;
A flattering painter, who made it his care
To draw men as they ought to be, not as they are.
His gallants are all faultless, his women divine,   65
And comedy wonders at being so fine;
Like a tragedy queen he has dizen'd her out,
Or rather like tragedy giving a rout.
His fools have their follies so lost in a crowd
Of virtues and feelings, that folly grows proud;   70
And coxcombs, alike in their failings alone,
Adopting his portraits, are pleas'd with their own.
Say, where has our poet this malady caught,
Or wherefore his characters thus without fault?
Say, was it that vainly directing his view   75
To find out men's virtues, and finding them few,
Quite sick of pursuing each troublesome elf,
He grew lazy at last, and drew from himself?

Here Douglas retires from his toils to relax,
The scourge of impostors, the terror of quacks: 80
Come, all ye quack bards, and ye quacking divines,
Come, and dance on the spot where your tyrant reclines:
When satire and censure encircled his throne,
I fear'd for your safety, I fear'd for my own;
But now he is gone, and we want a detector,   85
Our Dodds shall be pious, our Kenricks shall lecture;
Macpherson write bombast, and call it a style;
Our Townshend make speeches, and I shall compile;
New Lauders and Bowers the Tweed shall cross over
No countryman living their tricks to discover;   90
Detection her taper shall quench to a spark,
And Scotchman meet Scotchman, and cheat in the dark.

Here lies David Garrick, describe me who can,
An abridgment of all that was pleasant in man;
As an actor, confest without rival to shine;   95
As a wit, if not first, in the very first line:
Yet, with talents like these, and an excellent heart,
The man had his failings, a dupe to his art.
Like an ill-judging beauty, his colours he spread,
And beplaster'd with rouge his own natural red.   100
On the stage he was natural, simple, affecting;
'T was only that when he was off, he was acting.
With no reason on earth to go out of his way,
He turn'd and he varied full ten times a day:
Though secure of our hearts, yet confoundedly sick   105
If they were not his own by finessing and trick.
He cast off his friends, as a huntsman his pack;
For he knew, when he pleas'd, he could whistle them back.
Of praise a mere glutton, he swallow'd what came,
And the puff of a dunce he mistook it for fame;   110

Till his relish grown callous, almost to disease,
Who pepper'd the highest was surest to please.
But let us be candid, and speak out our mind,
If dunces applauded, he paid them in kind.
Ye Kenricks, ye Kellys, and Woodfalls so grave,   115
What a commerce was yours, while you got and you gave!
How did Grub-street re-echo the shouts that you rais'd,
While he was be-Roscius'd and you were beprais'd!
But peace to his spirit, wherever it flies,
To act as an angel, and mix with the skies.   120
Those poets who owe their best fame to his skill,
Shall still be his flatterers, go where he will;
Old Shakespeare receive him with praise and with love,
And Beaumonts and Bens be his Kellys above.

Here Hickey reclines, a most blunt, pleasant creature,   125
And slander itself must allow him good nature;
He cherish'd his friend, and he relish'd a bumper,
Yet one fault he had, and that one was a thumper.
Perhaps you may ask if the man was a miser:
I answer, No, no, for he always was wiser.   130
Too courteous, perhaps, or obligingly flat?
His very worst foe can't accuse him of that.
Perhaps he confided in men as they go,
And so was too foolishly honest? Ah, no!
Then what was his failing? come, tell it, and burn ye: 135
He was—could he help it?—a special attorney.

Here Reynolds is laid, and, to tell you my mind,
He has not left a wiser or better behind.
His pencil was striking, resistless, and grand;
His manners were gentle, complying, and bland: 140
Still born to improve us in every part,

His pencil our faces, his manners our heart.
To coxcombs averse, yet most civilly steering,
When they judg'd without skill, he was still hard of hearing:
When they talk'd of their Raphaels, Correggios, and stuff,
He shifted his trumpet, and only took snuff.   146
By flattery unspoil'd————

POSTSCRIPT

HERE Whitefoord reclines, and deny it who can,
Though he merrily liv'd, he is now a grave man:
Rare compound of oddity, frolic, and fun!   150
Who relish'd a joke, and rejoic'd in a pun;
Whose temper was generous, open, sincere;
A stranger to flattery, a stranger to fear;
Who scatter'd around wit and humour at will;
Whose daily *bon mots* half a column might fill: 155
A Scotchman, from pride and from prejudice free,
A scholar, yet surely no pedant was he.

NOTES ON GRAY'S POEMS

ELEGY WRITTEN IN A COUNTRY CHURCH-YARD—
(PAGE 3)

The *Elegy* was probably begun in 1742 and was finished at Stoke Pogis in June, 1750. Gray's mother and aunt lived here, and he was accustomed to come over from Cambridge frequently to spend a few days with them. His favorite walks are still pointed out. All three are buried in the church-yard, and there is a large monument to Gray in Stoke Park near by.

The poem may have been inspired by the death of Gray's dearest friend, Richard West. See Gosse, *Life of Gray*. The poet was in no haste to publish it and did so only to prevent an unauthorized edition. The piece almost immediately became very popular. It was translated into several languages and freely parodied. The author at first withheld his name and was always somewhat annoyed by the notoriety the poem brought him. He would accept no royalty for it. It should be read aloud and re-read until the remarkable beauty of expression, which has made it a universal favorite, is fully appreciated. It would be well to compare Bryant's *Thanatopsis* and Milton's *L'Allegro* and *Il Penseroso*.

1–12. What is the purpose of these introductory stanzas?

1. The curfew tolls. Thomas Carte, an historian contemporary with Gray, says that William the Conqueror instituted an ordinance, that all the common people should put out their fire and candle and go to bed at seven o'clock, upon the ringing of a bell, called the *couvre feu* bell, on pain of death.

Parting. Cf. *Deserted Village*, 171; also Longfellow's Dante, *Purgatory*, Canto VIII, 5, 6.

2. Wind. Why not *winds?*

4. And leaves the world. Cf. *Ode to Evening* by Collins and by Joseph Warton.

6. Holds. What is the subject?

7. Cf. *Lycidas,* 28, and *Macbeth*, Act III, sc. ii.

7–10. What is the effect of the sounds in these lines?

11. Bow'r. Meaning?

21. For them no more, etc. Cf. Burns's *The Cotter's Saturday Night*, 24–25, and 43–44; also Thomson's *Winter*, 311 ff.

27. Drive their team afield. Cf. *Lycidas*, 27. Milton's influence on Gray is very marked.

29–32. This stanza is used as the motto of *The Cotter's Saturday Night*. Note Gray's personifications.

33–36. Wolfe is said to have quoted these lines before the battle of Quebec, in which he was killed. See Parkman, *Montcalm and Wolfe*, II, 285.

37. Nor you, ye proud, etc. The poet had in mind some great cathedral like St. Paul's, in London.

43. Provoke. Look up the derivation.

46. Pregnant with celestial fire. Divinely inspired.

50. Why *spoils?*

51. Page. Meaning?

52. Genial. Meaning? Find the derivation.

57–60. Hampden, Milton, Cromwell. Originally Cato, Tully, and Cæsar. Why did Gray change? John Hampden lived not far from Stoke. Milton also resided for a time at Chalfont St. Giles, a short distance from Stoke Pogis, and finished *Paradise Lost* there. Cromwell was not yet understood in Gray's time.

72. The following stanzas originally appeared here. Should Gray have omitted them?

> The thoughtless world to Majesty may bow,
>   Exalt the brave, and idolize success;
> But more to innocence their safety owe,
>   Than Pow'r, or Genius, e'er conspir'd to bless.
>
> And thou, who mindful of th' unhonoured Dead,
>   Dost in these notes their artless tale relate,
> By night and lonely contemplation led
>   To wander in the gloomy walks of fate:
>
> Hark! how the sacred Calm, that breathes around
>   Bids every fierce tumultuous passion cease;
> In still small accents whispering from the ground,
>   A grateful earnest of eternal peace.
>
> No more, with reason and thyself at strife,
>   Give anxious cares and endless wishes room;
> But through the cool sequestered vale of life
>   Pursue the silent tenor of thy doom.

73. Thomas Hardy got the title for one of his novels from this line. Why the comma after *strife?*

78. Still. Meaning?

81. The tombstones in old grave-yards often have blundering epitaphs. It is so at Stoke.

85–88. What is the meaning of this stanza? What words are used with unusual meanings?

93–96. Cf. the second of the rejected stanzas, quoted in note to l. 72. What reminders here of Milton?

100. Lawn. Meaning? Cf. *Deserted Village*, 35.

After this stanza in the first manuscript followed these lines:

> Him have we seen the greenwood side along,
> While o'er the heath we hied, our labour done,
> Oft as the woodlark pip'd her farewell song,
> With wistful eyes pursue the setting sun.

105–112. These lines are inscribed on the monument to Gray in Stoke Park.

115. For thou canst read. What possible meanings?

116. After this stanza Gray originally wrote:

> There scatter'd oft, the earliest of the year,
> By hands unseen are show'rs of violets found;
> The redbreast loves to build and warble there,
> And little footsteps lightly print the ground.

Find what Lowell says about these lines in his *Essay on Gray*.

118. When did this cease to apply to Gray?

119. Science. Here means knowledge; cf. line 49.

Where are Gray's sympathies throughout the poem? Think of the various reasons why the poem should have become popular.

ODE ON A DISTANT PROSPECT OF ETON COLLEGE
—(Page 8)

This poem was written in August, 1742, when Gray was in his twenty-sixth year. He had returned from his travels, his father and his friend, Richard West, had died, and he was unsettled as to his future. He was visiting his mother at Stoke, where, by a short walk, he could ascend a hill and have a good view of the college which he had attended and of the surrounding country. The poem reflects the mood of pensive reflection which seems to have been frequent with the author. Compare Arnold's *The Scholar-Gypsy* and *Rugby Chapel*.

The motto from Menander, a Greek writer of comedies in the fourth century B.C., may be translated: "To be a man is reason enough to expect ill-fortune."

1. Imagine the view of Eton, Windsor Castle, and the Thames.

3. Science. Knowledge, as in the *Elegy*, l. 119.

4. Henry's. Henry VI, called Holy King Henry by Shakespeare, founded Eton College.

6. Find a picture of Windsor. Queen Victoria, Prince Albert, and Edward VII are buried here.

9. **Hoary Thames.** Rivers are often thought of as old. How did the Thames appear to the observer?

12. **Fields belov'd in vain.** His friend and companion, Richard West, had just died.

25-30. Gray himself took little part in these sports.

32. **Murm'ring labours.** Studying aloud.

39. **They hear a voice.** Whose?

55. The abbreviation *'em* was in good use in Gray's time.

60. Cf. the motto.

61. Note the members of Misfortune's train.

ODE ON THE DEATH OF A FAVOURITE CAT—(PAGE 11)

The following letter from Gray to his friend Walpole, which was written at Cambridge, March 1, 1747, explains the occasion of this ode and suggests the point of view. Walpole seems to have appreciated it, for after Gray's death he had the China Vase placed on a pedestal at Strawberry Hill, with a few lines from the ode upon it.

"As one ought to be particularly careful to avoid blunders in a compliment of condolence, it would be a sensible satisfaction to me (before I testify my sorrow, and the sincere part I take in your misfortune) to know for certain who it is I lament. I knew Zara and Selima (Selima was it? or Fatima?), or rather I knew them both together; for I cannot justly say which was which. Then as to your handsome Cat, the name you distinguish her by, I am no less at a loss, as well knowing one's handsome cat is always the cat one likes best; or if one be alive and the other dead, it is usually the latter that is the handsomest. Besides, if the point were never so clear, I hope you do not think me so ill-bred or so imprudent as to forfeit all my interest in the survivor; oh no! I would rather seem to mistake, and imagine to be sure it must be the tabby one that met with this sad accident. . . . Heigh ho! I feel (as you to be sure have done long since) that I have very little to say, at least in prose. Somebody will be the better for it; I do not mean you, but your Cat, feuë Mademoiselle Selime, whom I am about to immortalise for one week or fortnight, as follows."

2. **China's gayest art.** Europe learned from China the art of porcelain-making.

6. **Gaz'd on the lake.** Note the mock-heroic style throughout the poem.

12. **She saw.** Find the story of Narcissus in Gayley's *Classic Myths*.

16. **Tyrian hue.** Purple of Tyre.

20-22. The lines show that Gray has his "eye on the object."

31. **Eight times.** Cats have nine lives, according to the old superstition.

34. No Dolphin came. Find the story of Arion in Gayley's *Classic Myths*.

42. A proverb, merely quoted by Gray.

THE PROGRESS OF POESY—(PAGE 13)

This ode was written at Cambridge in 1754. In company with *The Bard*, it was first printed by Walpole on his press at Strawberry Hill in 1757. Gray called both pieces Pindaric odes, which means that he attempted to carry over into English the form and something of the spirit of the Greek poet Pindar. He was not the first to attempt this, but he was certainly the most successful. The first edition of the odes contained few notes. As Walpole feared, they proved "a little obscure," and Gray reluctantly added a number of explanations, which are generally considered necessary to a correct understanding of the odes. Most of these are reproduced below. For the classical references the student should consult Gayley's *Classic Myths*, or some other good dictionary of Classic Mythology.

The Pindaric ode has a definite and somewhat complex structure. As the numbers of the stanzas indicate, there are three groups of three each, and the corresponding members of these groups are exactly alike in structure. The reader should make out for himself the correspondences. The stanzas are called **Turn, Counter-Turn** and **After Song.**

The motto may be read in English: "They have a voice for the wise, but for the multitude they need interpreters." Gray did not expect a large audience for his odes.

1. "Pindar styles his own poetry, with its musical accompaniments, Æolian song, Æolian strings, the breath of the Æolian flute." —GRAY. The author quotes in connection with this line *Psalms* lvii. 8: "Awake, my glory; awake, lute and harp." What mistake did he make?

7. Note how sound corresponds with sense.

13. "Power of harmony to calm the turbulent sallies of the soul. The thoughts are borrowed from the first Pythian of Pindar."— GRAY.

15. Shell. See origin of the lyre in Gayley's *Classic Myths*. Lowell has a poem on it.

17. Lord of War. Mars. See Gayley's *Classic Myths*; cf. Chaucer, *Knight's Tale*, 1114 ff.

21. Feather'd king. The eagle, sacred to Zeus. See Gayley's *Classic Myths*.

25 Power of harmony to produce all the graces of motion in the body."—GRAY.

29. **Cytherea's.** See Gayley.

31. Cf. Milton's *L'Allegro.*

22. "To compensate the real and imaginary ills of life, the Muse was given to mankind by the same Providence that sends the day, by its cheerful presence, to dispel the gloom and terrors of the night." —GRAY.

46. **Fond.** Foolish.

50. **Birds of boding cry.** Screech-owls.

53. **Hyperion.** The sun. See Gayley.

54. "Extension of poetic genius over the remotest and most uncivilized nations: its connection with liberty and the virtues that nautrally attend on it."—GRAY.

66. "Progress of Poetry from Greece to Italy, and from Italy to England."—GRAY.

68. **Ilissus.** A river which flows through Athens.

69. **Maeander.** A river in Phrygia. Its winding course gave us our verb.

82. Note why the Muses passed on to England.

84. **Nature's darling.** "Shakespeare."—GRAY. Cf. *L'Allegro.*

95. **Nor second He.** Gray places Milton beside Shakespeare.

99. Cf. Ezekiel i. 28.

106. "This verse and the foregoing are meant to express the stately march and sounding energy of Dryden's rhymes."—GRAY.

111. "We have had in our language no other odes of the sublime kind, than that of Dryden on St. Cecilia's Day."—GRAY.

115. **Theban Eagle.** "Pindar compares himself to that bird."— GRAY.

121. Note Gray's idea of his own character and aims.

THE BARD—(PAGE 18)

This ode was begun in 1754 and finished in 1757. The argument is set down in Gray's commonplace book as follows: "The army of Edward I. as they march through a deep valley, are suddenly stopped by the appearance of a venerable figure seated on the summit of an inaccessible rock, who, with a voice more than human, reproaches the King with all the misery and desolation which he had brought on his country; foretells the misfortunes of the Norman race, and with prophetic spirit declares, that all his cruelty shall never extinguish the noble ardour of poetic genius in this island; and that men shall never be wanting to celebrate true virtue and valour in immortal strains, to expose vice and infamous pleasure, and boldly censure tyranny and oppression. His song ended, he precipitates himself from the mountain, and is swallowed up by the river that rolls at its foot."

Gray may have got his idea of Edward's persecution of the Welsh bards from Carte, who says: "The only set of men among the Welsh, that had reason to complain of Edward's severity, were the bards who used to put those of the ancient Britons in mind of the valiant deeds of their ancestors: he ordered them all to be hanged, as inciters of the people to sedition." There is, however, no evidence of a general massacre of the bards.

1. Picture the scene.

2. Confusion. Destruction.

4. Cf. *King John*, V. i. 72.

8. Cambria's. Latin for *Cymri*, land of the Kymry (or Welsh).

12. King Edward conquered Wales in 1282–84.

18. Haggard. Wild, a metaphor from hawking.

28. High-born Hoël. A Welsh warrior and poet.

29. Cadwallo. A Welsh poet.

33. Modred. Not he of the King Arthur tales.

35. They lie. The bards who had been slaughtered.

40. Cf. *Julius Cæsar*, II. i. 289.

44. Grisly band. Ghosts of the bards.

47. Note that lines 49–100 are spoken by the chorus of dead bards in unison with the original speaker. After that the one singer continues alone, the spirits having vanished.

49. Warp and woof. Meaning?

51. Verge. Meaning?

54. Severn. The river.

55. Berkley's roofs. A Norman castle, still well preserved. Edward II was killed here.

57. She-wolf of France. Isabel of France, queen of Edward II.

61. Amazement. Bewilderment, as in Shakespeare.

67. Sable warrior. "Edward the Black Prince."—GRAY.

71. "Magnificence of Richard the Second's reign. See Froissart, and other contemporary writers."—GRAY.

79–81. Alluding to the deposition and death of Richard II.

83. "Ruinous civil wars of York and Lancaster."—GRAY.

87. "Henry the Sixth, George Duke of Clarence, Edward the Fifth, Richard Duke of York, etc., believed to be murdered secretly in the Tower of London. The oldest part of that structure is vulgarly attributed to Julius Cæsar."—GRAY.

89. "Margaret of Anjou, a woman of heroic spirit, who struggled hard to save her husband and her crown; Henry the Fifth."—GRAY.

90. "Henry the Sixth, very near being canonized. The line of Lancaster had no right of inheritance to the crown."—GRAY.

91. "The white and red roses, devices of York and Lancaster."—GRAY.

93. "The silver boar was the badge of Richard the Third; whence he was usually known in his own time by the name of the Boar."—GRAY.

99. **Half of thy heart.** Edward's wife, Eleanor, saved his life by sucking the venom from the wound made by a poisoned dagger. She died in 1290.

101. **Stay, oh stay!** On whom does the bard call?

105. **But oh!** The bard has a vision of better times to come.

109. **Long-lost Arthur.** "It was the common belief of the Welsh nation, that King Arthur was still alive in Fairy-Land, and should return again to reign over Britain."—GRAY.

110. "Both Merlin and Taliessin had prophesied that the Welsh should regain their sovereignty over this island; which seemed to be accomplished in the house of Tudor."—GRAY. How?

117. **Her lion-port.** Is this picture of Elizabeth correct?

121. **Taliessin.** A Welsh poet, a few of whose poems have come down to us.

126. Cf. the dedication to Spenser's *Faerie Queene.*

127. **Buskined.** Tragic. How did the term originate?

131. "Milton."—GRAY.

133. "The succession of poets after Milton's time."—GRAY.

140. **The different doom.** The house of Edward is to be destroyed; the bard is to triumph in the accession of the Tudors.

Once in possession of the necessary information, the student should read the poem aloud, seeking to realize its dramatic quality. For other examples of the ode, see Gosse, *English Odes.*

NOTES ON GOLDSMITH'S POEMS

THE DESERTED VILLAGE—(Page 27)

The *Traveller* is Goldsmith's earliest poem, but the *Deserted Village* is the best introduction to him and is here placed first. The poem was published in 1770, when the writer was at his best and already popular. It ran through five editions in three months and has always been a favorite. Goethe found it a poetical production which his little circle "hailed with transport." Sir Joshua Reynolds, to whom the piece was dedicated, responded by painting a picture called *Resignation*, upon which he caused to be engraved the following: "This attempt to express a character in the *Deserted Village* is dedicated to Doctor Goldsmith, by his sincere friend and admirer, Joshua Reynolds." Gray said: "This man is a poet." The poem is full of genuine human sympathy and contains much of beauty, pathos, and grace. It is of small moment that the conditions which Goldsmith described are partly imaginary and that his philosophy is somewhat at fault. The spirit is right.

1. Sweet Auburn. Goldsmith may have had his boyhood home at Lissoy, Ireland, in mind; but the scenes are highly idealized and not to be identified exactly with any one village, Irish or other.

5. Note the yearning tenderness with which Goldsmith paints these pictures of happy country life which he was never again to share.

12. Decent. In the old meaning, becoming.

17. Train. Note Goldsmith's fondness for this word.

19. Circled. Cf. line 22.

23. Still. Meaning?

27. The reference is to the old trick of inducing the victim to make signs on his face while holding an object blackened on the under surface. For a description of these rude sports see the Chapter *A London Suburb* in Hawthorne's *Our Old Home*.

44. In his *Animated Nature*, Goldsmith speaks of the dismally hollow booming of the bittern. "I remember," he says, "in the place where I was a boy, with what terror this bird's note affected the whole village."

51. Cf. *The Traveller*, 303 ff. and *The Vicar of Wakefield*, Chap. xix.

74. Manners. Meaning?

83, 84. To what experiences does Goldsmith refer in these lines?

124. It is said that the nightingale is not found in Ireland.

141. See the dedication to *The Traveller*, page 43. Cf. the description of the poor parson in Chaucer's *Prologue*.

196. The Village Master. The original is said to be Goldsmith's early master Thomas Byrne. Cf. Whittier's picture of an early teacher in his *Snow-Bound*.

209. Terms. Sessions of the law courts. **Tides** were times or seasons, especially those of the ecclesiastical year. Cf. Eastertide.

232. The twelve good rules ascribed to Charles I are: 1. Urge no healths. 2. Profane no divine ordinances. 3. Touch no state matters. 4. Reveal no secrets. 5. Pick no quarrels. 6. Make no companions. 7. Maintain no ill opinions. 8. Keep no bad company. 9. Encourage no vice. 10. Make no long meal. 11. Repeat no grievances. 12. Lay no wagers.

232. The royal game of goose was a kind of checkers.

244. Woodman. Probably a hunter rather than a wood-chopper.

250. On this custom see *Marmion*, Canto V, stanza 12, and Ben Jonson's "Drink to me only with thine eyes."

265. Are the evils of which Goldsmith complains unheard of to-day?

316. Artist. In Goldsmith's time this word was applied to any worker in the mechanic arts.

322. Chariots. Carriages. **Torches** were borne by link-boys to light the way.

343–359. Like most Englishmen, even of a later day, Goldsmith had very incorrect notions of American geography. Note his choice of a name which he could fit into his verse.—*Altama* means Altamaha.

368. Seats. Homes.

397. Goldsmith sees in vision an emigrant band leaving England for America.

418. Torno. Probably the river Tornea or Torneo, which flows into the Gulf of Bothnia. Pambamarca is a mountain near Quito. What idea does the poet wish to bring out?

427–430. We learn from Boswell that these lines were added by Dr. Johnson. Do they sound like the remainder of the poem?

As you re-read the poem, note the succession of moods. What

memorable lines have you noticed? Is there any likeness to Gray's *Elegy?*

THE TRAVELLER—(Page 43)

Goldsmith began *The Traveller* in Switzerland in 1755 while on his travels, but did not complete it until 1764. It was the first of his works to be published with his name, and hence laid the foundation of his reputation as a writer. The other members of the Literary Club were astonished that he should have produced so good a poem, and at once began to hold him in high esteem. Dr. Johnson always regarded the piece as superior to the *Deserted Village.* The world has not agreed with him, but it has nevertheless accorded the *Traveller* high praise.

The order of treatment is practically that of the places visited, and, therefore, the whole constitutes a sort of poetic record of the writer's impressions, though it contains a fundamental philosophic view which serves to unify it. The social contrasts, which, in the *Deserted Village* are presented as appearing within a single country, are here drawn between different countries, with the Englishman's preference for his own clearly indicated. But the underlying idea is that happiness depends upon the individual and not upon the country or kind of government in which he finds himself.

1. Boswell reports that at a meeting of the Literary Club shortly after the publication of the poem, Chamier said to Goldsmith: "What do you mean by the last word in the first line of your *Traveller?* Do you mean tardiness of locomotion?" "Yes," replied Goldsmith. But Johnson interposed, saying: "No sir, you did not mean tardiness of locomotion; you meant that sluggishness of mind which comes upon a man in solitude." "Ah," exclaimed Goldsmith, "*that* was what I meant!" The incident caused a rumor that Johnson had written many of the best lines of the poem, but Johnson himself set this at rest by marking those he did write—the 420th and the last ten lines, except the 435th and 436th.

3. Carinthia is a province of Austria east of the Tyrol, which Goldsmith visited in 1755. It was noted for inhospitality.

5. Campania. Probably the Roman Campagna is meant.

10. See *Citizen of the World*, Letter III, and Irving's *The Voyage* in the *Sketch-Book.*

13–22. Cf. *The Deserted Village*, 149–152.

23. Me. Object of *leads* in line 29.

24, 27. Why the dashes?

33. Cf. *The Deserted Village*, 188–190.

48. Dress. Cf. *Genesis* ii. 15.

60. Real. Two syllables.

69. Line. Equator. Cf. Tennyson's *Enoch Arden*, 601.

84. Idra. A mountainous district of Austria. **Arno.** A river in Italy.

86. Explain the meaning of this line.

87. Art in the broad sense.

92. Cf. the idea of commerce in *The Deserted Village*.

68. Peculiar, to itself.

99. What is the purpose of this paragraph?

118. Vernal lives. Meaning?

127. Manners. Cf. *The Deserted Village*, 74.

134, 5. The Italian republics, Venice, Genoa, Florence, and Pisa, were at the height of their prosperity in the fifteenth century.

136. Long-fall'n. Since the palmy days of Rome. Goldsmith is here referring to the Italian Renaissance.

140. Because of the discovery of the route around the Cape of Good Hope.

150. Pasteboard triumph. Carnival shows.

159. Cf. *The Deserted Village*, 319.

167. Bleak Mansion. Meaning?

170. Man and Steel. The Swiss were frequently employed as mercenaries in the seventeenth and eighteenth centuries; see Carlyle's *French Revolution*, chap. vii, bk. ii.

194. Cf. the *Elegy*, 21.

198. Nightly. For the night.

234. Cowering. Brooding. There is no idea of fear.

243. Cf. *Vicar of Wakefield*, chap. xx.

253. Gestic lore. Skill in the dance.

276. Frieze. Coarse cloth brought originally from Friesland.

297. Wave-subjected. Meaning?

306. Possibly a reference to the selling of children's labor for a term of years.

309. Is Goldsmith's attack on the Dutch justified?

319. Scorn Arcadian pride. Are superior to lawns that would be the pride of Arcadia—an imaginary country of perfect pastoral beauty.

320. Hydaspes. The Jelum, a branch of the Indus.

327. Port. Cf. *The Bard*, 117.

357. Stems. Families.

382–392. Cf. *Vicar of Wakefield*, chap. xix. Goldsmith seems to have had an aversion to republics.

388. The allusion is probably to Englishmen who used their wealth acquired in the East to buy their way into Parliament; perhaps specially to Lord Clive, who was elected to Parliament in 1761. See Macaulay's *Essay on Clive.*

397. Cf. *The Deserted Village,* 275 ff.

412. The pronunciation of Niagara required by the metre is still common in England.

411. Oswego. Cf. his choice of Altama in *The Deserted Village,* 344.

436. Luke's iron crown. Two brothers, George and Luke Dosa, in 1514 led a revolt against the Hungarian nobles, and George was proclaimed king. For this he (not Luke) was tortured with a red-hot crown. Damiens attempted the assassination of Louis XV of France and was put to death in the most barbarous manner possible.

RETALIATION—(Page 61)

This poem was published after Goldsmith's death. It was occasioned by the attempts of Goldsmith's associates to make fun at his expense. Garrick, the great actor, wrote an account of it, in which he says that in response to a challenge to try his powers of epigram he spoke the following extempore lines as Goldsmith's epitaph:

> Here lies Nolly Goldsmith, for shortness call'd Noll,
> Who wrote like an angel, but talk'd like poor Poll.

Goldsmith was unable to respond at the time, but afterward wrote this poem. It is full of fine characterizations and may be compared with Lowell's *Fable for Critics.*

1. Scarron. A French comic writer.

3. The friends had dined at St. James's Coffee-house.

5. Thomas Barnard, Dean of Derry in Ireland.

6. Edmund Burke.

7. William Burke, kinsman of Edmund.

8. Richard Burke, brother of Edmund.

9. Richard Cumberland, a dramatist and essayist of importance in his day.

10. John Douglas, a prominent ecclesiastic.

14. John Ridge, of the Irish Bar.

15. Thomas Hickey, an attorney and general favorite in the circle.

34. Thomas Townshend, member of Parliament.

54. Richard Burke had broken his leg.

86. The line rhymes with the previous one. Mr. Dodds was a preacher who turned out badly. Kenrick a hack-writer of the period who had lectured on Shakespeare, was an enemy of Goldsmith.

87. Look up James Macpherson in a history of English literature.

115. **Kenrick,** a critic and enemy of Goldsmith, **Kelly,** a dramatist whose sentimental comedy, *False Delicacy*, had a brief fame, and **Woodhull,** an editor, were all representative flatterers of Garrick.

117. Poor authors lived on Grub-street.

124. Beaumont and Ben Jonson were long ranked second only to Shakespeare.

147. Goldsmith died, leaving the poem unfinished.

148. The so-called Postscript consists of lines found after four editions of the remainder had been printed. **Whitefoord** was a wine merchant.

---

rnold's Sohrab and Rustum and Other Poems.
Edited by Ashley H. Thorndike, Professor of English in Columbia University. $0.25. [For Reading.]

rowning's Select Poems.
Edited by Percival Chubb, Director of English, Ethical Culture Schools, New York. $0.25. [For Reading.]

unyan's Pilgrim's Progress.
Edited by Charles Sears Baldwin, Professor of Rhetoric in Yale University. $0.25. [For Reading.]

urke's Speech on Conciliation with America.
Edited by Albert S. Cook, Professor of the English.Language and Literature in Yale University. $0.25. [For Study.]

yron's Childe Harold, Canto IV, and Prisoner of Chillon.
Edited by H. E. Coblentz, Principal of The South Division High School, Milwaukee, Wis. $0.25. [For Reading.]

arlyle's Essay on Burns.
Edited by Wilson Farrand, Principal of the Newark Academy, Newark, N. J., $0.25. [For Study.]

arlyle's Heroes, Hero-Worship, and the Heroic in History.
Edited by Henry David Gray, Instructor in English in Leland Stanford, Jr. University. $0.25. [For Reading.]

Coleridge's The Rime of the Ancient Mariner.
Edited by Herbert Bates, Brooklyn Manual Training High School, New York. $0.25. [For Reading.]

DeQuincey's Joan of Arc and The English Mail Coach.
Edited by Charles Sears Baldwin, Professor of Rhetoric in Yale University. $0.25. [For Reading, 1910 to 1912.]

Dickens's A Tale of Two Cities.
Edited by Frederick William Roe, Assistant Professor of English, Univ. of Wisconsin. $0.25. [For Reading.]

Franklin's Autobiography.
Edited by William B. Cairns, Assistant Professor of American Literature in the University of Wisconsin. $0.25. [For Reading.]

Gaskell's Cranford.
Edited by Franklin T. Baker, Professor of the English Language and Literature in Teachers College, Columbia University. $0.25. [For Reading.]

George Eliot's Silas Marner.
Edited by Robert Herrick, Professor of Rhetoric in the University of Chicago. $0.25. [For Reading.]

Goldsmith's The Vicar of Wakefield.
Edited by Mary A. Jordan, Professor of Rhetoric and Old English in Smith College. $0.25. [For Reading.]

Gray's Elegy In A Country Churchyard and Goldsmith's The Deserted Village.
Edited by James F. Hosic, Head of the Department of English in the Chicago Normal School, Chicago, Ill. $0.25. [For Reading.]

Huxley's Autobiography and Selections From Lay Sermons.
Edited by E. H. Kemper McComb, Head of the Department of English in the Manual Training High School, Indianapolis, Ind. $0.25. [For Reading.]

Irving's Sketch Book.
With an Introduction by Brander Matthews, Professor of Dramatic Literature, Columbia University, and with notes by Armour Caldwell, A.B. $0.25. [For Reading.]

Lincoln, Selections From.
Edited by Daniel K. Dodge, Professor of English in the University of Illinois. $0.25. [For Reading.]

Lowell's Vision of Sir Launfal, and Other Poems.
Edited by Allan Abbott, Head of the Department of English, Horace Mann High School, Teachers College, New York City. $0.25. [For Reading.]

Macaulay's Essay on Lord Clive.
Edited by Preston C. Farrar, Instructor of English in Erasmus Hall High School, Brooklyn, N. Y. $0.25. [For Reading.]

Macaulay's Lays of Ancient Rome, with Ivry and The Armada.
Edited by Nott Flint, late Instructor in English in the University of Chicago. $0.25. [For Reading.]

Macaulay's Life of Samuel Johnson.
Edited by Huber Gray Buehler, Head-master Hotchkiss School, Lakeville, Conn. $0.25. [For Study.]

Macaulay's Warren Hastings.
Edited by Samuel M. Tucker, Professor of English and Dean in The Florida State College. $0.25. [For Reading.]

Milton's L'Allegro, Il Penseroso, Comus and Lycidas.
Edited by William P. Trent, Professor of English Literature in Columbia University. $0.25. [For Study; after 1911, "Lycidas" is omitted.]

Parkman's The Oregon Trail.
Edited by Ottis B. Sperlin, Head of the Department of English in the Tacoma High School, Washington. $0.25. [For Reading.]

Palgrave's The Golden Treasury.
Edited by Herbert Bates, of the Manual Training High School, Brooklyn, New York City. $0.25. [For Reading.]

Ruskin's Sesame and Lilies.
Edited by Gertrude Buck, Associate Professor of English in Vassar College. $0.25. [For Reading.]

Scott's Ivanhoe.
Edited by Bliss Perry, Professor of English Literature in Harvard University. $0.25. [For Reading.]

Scott's Lady of the Lake.
Edited by George Rice Carpenter, late Professor of Rhetoric and English Composition in Columbia University. $0.25. [For Reading.]

Scott's Quentin Durward.
Edited by Mary E. Adams, Head of the Department of English in the Central High School, Cleveland, O. $0.25. [For Reading.]

Shakspere's A Midsummer Night's Dream.
Edited by George Pierce Baker, Professor of English in Harvard University. $0.25. [For Reading.]

Shakspere's As You Like It.
With an Introduction by Barrett Wendell, A.B., Professor of English in Harvard University; and Notes by William Lyon Phelps, Lampson Professor of English Literaure in Yale University. $0.25. [For Reading.]

Shakspere's Macbeth.
Edited by John Matthews Manly, Professor and Head of the Department of English in the University of Chicago. $0.25. [For Study.]

Shakspere's Julius Caesar.
Edited by George C. D. Odell, Professor of English in Columbia University. $0.25. [For Reading.]

Shakspere's King Henry V.
Edited by George C. D. Odell, Professor of English in Columbia University. $0.25. [For Reading.]

Shakspere's The Merchant of Venice.
Edited by Francis B. Gummere, Professor of English in Haverford College. $0.25. [For Reading.]

Shakspere's Twelfth Night.
Edited by John B. Henneman, Ph.D., late Professor of English in the University of the South. $0.25. [For Reading.]

Spenser's The Faerie Queene. (Selections.)
Edited by John Erskine, Professor of English in Amherst College. $0.25. [For Reading.]

Stevenson's Treasure Island.
Edited by Clayton Hamilton, Extension Lecturer in English, Columbia University $0.25. [For Reading.]

Tennyson's Gareth and Lynette, Lancelot and Elaine, The Passing of Arthur.
Edited by Sophie C. Hart, Associate Professor of Rhetoric in Wellesley College. $0.25. [For Reading, 1909 to 1915. For Study, 1912.]

Tennyson's The Princess.
Edited by George Edward Woodberry, formerly Professor of Comparative Literature in Columbia University. $0.25. [For Reading, 1912.]

The Sir Roger de Coverley Papers.
Edited by D. O. S. Lowell, Head-master of the Roxbury Latin School, Boston, Mass. $0.25. [For Reading.]

Thoreau's Walden.
Edited by Raymond M. Alden, Professor of English in Leland Stanford Junior University, California. $0.25. [For Reading.]

Webster's First Bunker Hill Oration and Washington's Farewell Address.
Edited by Fred Newton Scott, Professor of Rhetoric in the University of Michigan. $0.25. [For Study.]

Cooper's The Last of the Mohicans.
Edited by Charles F. Richardson, Professor of English in Dartmouth College. $0.50.

Defoe's History of the Plague in London.
Edited by George R. Carpenter, late Professor of Rhetoric and English Composition in Columbia University. $0.60.

De Quincey's Flight of a Tartar Tribe.
Edited by Charles Sears Baldwin, Professor of Rhetoric in Yale University. $0.40.

Dryden's Palamon and Arcite.
Edited by William Tenney Brewster, Professor of English in Columbia University. $0.40.

Irving's Life of Goldsmith.
Edited by Lewis B. Semple, Instructor in English, Brooklyn Commercial High School, New York. $0.25.

Irving's Tales of a Traveller.
With an Introduction by Brander Matthews, Professor of Dramatic Literature in Columbia University, and Explanatory Notes by Professor George R. Carpenter. $0.80.

Macaulay's Essay on Milton.
Edited by James Greenleaf Croswell, Head-master of the Brearley School, New York. $0.40.

Macaulay's Essays on Milton and Addison.
Edited by James Greenleaf Croswell, Head-master of the Brearley School, New York. $0.40.

Macaulay's Johnson and Addison.
1. LIFE OF SAMUEL JOHNSON, edited by Huber Gray Buehler, Hotchkiss School.
2. ADDISON, edited by James Greenleaf Croswell, Brearley School. $0.40.

Milton's Paradise Lost. Books I. and II.
Edited by Edward Everett Hale, Jr., Professor of the English Language and Literature in Union College. $0.40.

Pope's Homer's Iliad. Books I., VI., XXII. and XXIV.
Edited by William H. Maxwell, Superintendent of New York City Schools; and Percival Chubb, Director of English in the Ethical Culture Schools, New York. $0.40.

Scott's Marmion.
Edited by Robert Morss Lovett, Professor of English in the University of Chicago. $0.60.

Scott's Woodstock.
Edited by Bliss Perry, Professor of English Literature in Harvard University. $0.60.

Southey's Life of Nelson.
Edited by Edwin L. Miller, Head of the English Department, Central High School, Detroit, Mich. $0.60.